HEART HEALTHY AND LOW CHOLESTEROL

For Beginners 2024

Delicious, Easy-To-Follow Recipes for A Stronger Heart And Promote Long-Term Well-Being With Comprehensive Advice and A 30-Day Meal Plan

Mharta Leuman

Copyright

© Copyright 2024: Mharta Leuman - All rights reserved.

The content contained within this book may not be reproduced, duplicated, or transmitted without direct written permission from the author or the publisher.

Under no circumstances will any blame or legal responsibility be held against the publisher, or author, for any damages, reparation, or monetary loss due to the information contained within this book. Either directly or indirectly.

Legal Notice:

This book is copyright protected. This book is only for personal use. You cannot amend, distribute, sell, use, quote, or paraphrase any part, or the content within this book, without the author's or publisher's consent.

Disclaimer Notice:

Please note the information contained within this document is for educational and entertainment purposes only. All effort has been executed to present accurate, up-to-date, and reliable, complete information. No warranties of any kind are declared or implied. Readers acknowledge that the author does not render legal, financial, medical, or professional advice. The content within this book has been derived from various sources. Please consult a licensed professional before attempting any techniques outlined in this book.

By reading this document, the reader agrees that under no circumstances is the author responsible for any direct or indirect losses incurred due to the use of the information contained within this document, including, but not limited to, errors, omissions, or inaccuracies.

Table of Contents

Part One
Theory and Information
Introduction

Welcome to "The Low Cholesterol Cookbook" 8
Book Overview 8
Importance of a Low-Cholesterol Diet 8
Objectives of the Book 8

Chapter 1
Understanding Cholesterol 9

1.1 What is Cholesterol? 9
    1.1.1 Definition of Cholesterol 9
    1.1.2 Types of Cholesterol: LDL and HDL 9
    1.1.3 Role of Triglycerides 9
    1.1.4 Mechanisms of Action of Cholesterol in the Body 9
    1.1.5 Effects of High Cholesterol on Arteries 9
    1.1.6 Impacts on Cardiovascular Health 9
1.2 Risk Factors and Causes of High Cholesterol 10
    1.2.1 Genetic Influence on Cholesterol 10
    1.2.2 Role of Diet in Cholesterol Management 10
    1.2.3 Lifestyle and Cholesterol 10
    1.2.4 Diabetes and Cholesterol 10
    1.2.5 Obesity and Metabolic Syndrome 10
    1.2.6 Other Medical Conditions 10
1.3 Benefits of Lowering Cholesterol 10
    1.3.1 Reduced Risk of Heart Attacks 10
    1.3.2 Improved Blood Circulation 10
    1.3.3 Reduction in Blood Pressure 10
    1.3.4 Decreased Risk of Stroke 11
    1.3.5 Prevention of Other Chronic Diseases 11
    1.3.6 Long-term Benefits 11

Chapter 2
Dietary Guidelines for Lowering Cholesterol 12

2.1 Foods to Avoid 12
    2.1.1 Common Sources of Saturated Fats 12
    2.1.2 Effects of Trans Fats on Cholesterol 12

- 2.1.3 Healthier Alternatives ... 12
- 2.1.4 How Sugars Affect Cholesterol ... 12
- 2.1.5 Avoiding Simple Carbohydrates ... 12
- 2.1.6 Healthier Choices of Carbohydrates ... 12
- 2.2 Foods to Include ... 12
  - 2.2.1 Benefits of Omega-3s ... 12
  - 2.2.2 Sources of Monounsaturated Fats ... 13
  - 2.2.3 How to Incorporate These Fats into the Diet ... 13
  - 2.2.4 Benefits of Soluble Fibers ... 13
  - 2.2.5 Importance of Fruits and Vegetables ... 13
  - 2.2.6 Legumes and Cholesterol ... 13
- 2.3 The Role of Physical Activity ... 13
  - 2.3.1 Aerobic Exercises ... 13
  - 2.3.2 Endurance Exercises ... 13
  - 2.3.3 Daily Physical Activities ... 13
  - 2.3.4 How Exercise Lowers Cholesterol ... 13
  - 2.3.5 Synergy Between Diet and Exercise ... 13
  - 2.3.6 Exercise Plan for Beginners ... 13

Chapter 3
Practical Cooking Tips ... 14

- 3.1 How to Read Nutrition Labels ... 14
  - 3.1.1 Energy Value and Portions ... 14
  - 3.1.2 Total Saturated and Trans Fats ... 14
  - 3.1.3 Added Sugars ... 14
  - 3.1.4 Common Names for Hidden Sugars and Fats ... 14
  - 3.1.5 Additives and Preservatives to Avoid ... 14
  - 3.1.6 Healthier Alternatives ... 14
- 3.2 Healthy Cooking Techniques ... 14
  - 3.2.1 Steaming ... 14
  - 3.2.2 Grilling and Baking ... 14
  - 3.2.3 Use of Non-Stick Cookware ... 15
  - 3.2.4 Benefits of Spices ... 15
  - 3.2.5 Create Spice Mixes ... 15
  - 3.2.6 Examples of Recipes with Spices ... 15
- 3.3 Meal Planning and Preparation ... 15
  - 3.3.1 Importance of Planning ... 15
  - 3.3.2 Sample Weekly Plan ... 15
  - 3.3.3 Tailor the Plan to Your Personal Needs ... 15
  - 3.3.4 Preparing Meals in Advance ... 15
  - 3.3.5 Food Storage ... 15
  - 3.3.6 Useful Tools for Meal Preparation ... 15

Chapter 4
Additional Resources ... 16

- 4.1 Glossary of Nutritional Terms ... 16
  - 4.1.1 Common Terms ... 16
  - 4.1.2 Detailed Explanations ... 16

  4.1.3 Practical Examples 16
 4.2 Digital Tools and Resources for a Low Cholesterol Diet 16
  4.2.1 Cholesterol Monitoring App 16
  4.2.2 Meal Planning Tools 16
  4.2.3 Forums and Online Support Communities 16
 4.3 Interactive Experiences and Bonus Material 16
  4.3.1 Food Awareness Quiz 16
  4.3.2 Healthy Shopping Checklist 17
  4.3.3 Tools to Monitor Progress 17
  4.3.4 Step-by-Step Cooking Videos 17
  4.3.5 Interviews with Nutrition Experts 17
  4.3.6 Guided Training Sessions 17

Part Two
Recipes

Breakfast 19
 1. Avocado Toast with Tomato and Chia Seeds 19
 3. Oatmeal Pancakes 20
 4. Greek Yogurt with Honey and Nuts 21
 5. Egg White Omelette with Spinach and Feta 21
 6. Quinoa Porridge with Dried Fruit 22
 7. Whole Wheat Bagel with Smoked Salmon and Avocado 22
 8. Vanilla Chia Pudding 23
 9. Carrot and Almond Muffins 24
 10. Whole Wheat Bread Toast with Almond Butter and Banana 25
 11. Green Detox Smoothie 26
 12. Yogurt Parfait with Granola and Fruit 26
 13. Whole Wheat Waffles with Fresh Fruit 27
 14. Tofu Scramble with Vegetables 28
 15. Overnight Oats with Chia Seeds and Fruit 29

Lunch Recipes 30
 1. Quinoa and Vegetable Salad 30
 2. Grilled Chicken Wrap 31
 3. Lentil Soup 32
 4. Chickpea and Spinach Salad 33
 5. Fish Tacos 34
 6. Grilled Chicken with Roasted Vegetables 35
 7. Spelt and Vegetable Salad 36
 8. Hummus & Vegetable Wrap 37
 9. Brown Rice with Vegetable Curry 38
 10. Baked Salmon with Asparagus 39
 11. Arugula and Avocado Salad 40
 12. Vegetable Minestrone 41
 13. Couscous and Chickpea Salad 42
 14. Turkey Meatballs with Tomato Sauce 43
 15. Barley Salad with Grilled Vegetables 44

Dinner Recipes 45
1. Baked Salmon with Asparagus 45
2. Lemon and Herb Chicken 46
3. Vegetable and Bean Soup 47
4. Tofu Stir-Fry with Vegetables 48
5. Spinach and Smoked Salmon Salad 49
6. Chicken Fajitas 50
7. Almond-Crusted Cod 51
8. Zucchini Spaghetti with Pesto 52
9. Turkey and Bean Chili 53
10. Risotto with Mushrooms 54
11. Lentil Meatballs 55
12. Chicken and Avocado Salad 56
13. Grilled Shrimp with Vegetables 57
14. Kale and Quinoa Salad 58
15. Baked Tofu with Vegetables 59

Snacks & Snacks 60
1. Low-Fat Chickpea Hummus 60
2. Green Smoothie 61
3. Dried Fruit Bars 62
4. Greek Yogurt with Honey and Nuts 63
5. Kale Chips 64
6. Fresh Fruit with Almond Butter 65
7. Steamed Edamame 66
8. Guacamole with Vegetable Sticks 67
9. Parmesan Popcorn 68
10. Fruit Salad 69

Dessert Recipes 70
1. Avocado Chocolate Mousse 70
2. Greek Yogurt and Berries Parfait 71
3. Black Bean Brownies 72
4. Banana Ice Cream 73
5. Coconut Chia Pudding 74
6. Whole Wheat Apple Pie 75
7. Blueberry Muffins 76
8. Fruit Crumble 77
9. Coconut Panna Cotta 78
10. Oat and Banana Cookies 79

Conclusion 80
Index 81
Bonus 84

Part One

Theory and Information Introduction

Welcome to "The Low Cholesterol Cookbook"

In a world where culinary delights often betray our health, welcome to "The Low Cholesterol Cookbook." This is not just a book; it is a journey into the heart of wholesome and indulgent cuisine. We embark on this journey with the understanding that our greatest asset, our health, deserves to be nurtured with the same passion and creativity we bring to the table. This book is your trusted companion, filled with recipes that are not only delightful but also crafted to support your heart health.

Book Overview

Within these pages, you will discover a treasure trove of recipes, each one a testament to the art of healthy cooking. The essence of this cookbook is to demystify the notion that healthy food cannot be delicious. Here, you will find an array of meals that are low in cholesterol yet brimming with flavor, creativity, and joy. From sumptuous breakfasts to satisfying dinners and delightful desserts, every recipe has been meticulously curated to ensure it aligns with a heart-healthy diet.

Importance of a Low-Cholesterol Diet

The significance of a low-cholesterol diet cannot be overstated. It is the keystone to a life of vitality, reduced risk of heart disease, and overall well-being. High cholesterol is a silent adversary, stealthily compromising our health. By embracing a diet low in cholesterol, we fortify our hearts, enhance our longevity, and embrace a life of vigor and wellness. This book is crafted with the intent to make this transition not only seamless but also enjoyable.

Objectives of the Book

The primary goal of "The Low Cholesterol Cookbook" is to provide you with the tools and inspiration needed to adopt and sustain a heart-healthy diet. We aim to transform your kitchen into a haven of healthful delights, where each meal is a step towards a healthier heart. Whether you are a culinary novice or a seasoned chef, this book offers practical guidance, mouthwatering recipes, and a compassionate understanding of the challenges and triumphs that come with dietary changes.

Chapter 1
Understanding Cholesterol

1.1 What is Cholesterol?

1.1.1 Definition of Cholesterol

Cholesterol, that enigmatic substance so often vilified, is in fact a crucial component of our being. It is a lipid, a waxy substance produced by our liver and obtained from certain foods. Cholesterol is essential for the formation of cell membranes, vitamin D, and certain hormones. However, its dual nature means that while it is vital for our health, an excess can be dangerous.

1.1.2 Types of Cholesterol: LDL and HDL

There are two principal types of cholesterol: Low-Density Lipoprotein (LDL) and High-Density Lipoprotein (HDL). LDL is often termed "bad" cholesterol, for it can lead to the buildup of plaques in our arteries, narrowing them and increasing the risk of heart disease. HDL, on the other hand, is known as "good" cholesterol, as it helps transport cholesterol away from the arteries and back to the liver, where it is processed and removed from the body.

1.1.3 Role of Triglycerides

Triglycerides are another type of lipid found in your blood. When you eat, your body converts any calories it doesn't need to use right away into triglycerides. High levels of triglycerides can increase the risk of heart disease, especially when combined with high LDL cholesterol and low HDL cholesterol levels.

1.1.4 Mechanisms of Action of Cholesterol in the Body

Cholesterol travels through the bloodstream in lipoproteins. LDL carries cholesterol to the cells, where it is used or stored. When there is too much LDL, it can deposit cholesterol in the artery walls, leading to atherosclerosis. HDL helps to counteract this by transporting cholesterol from the arteries to the liver for removal.

1.1.5 Effects of High Cholesterol on Arteries

High levels of LDL cholesterol can lead to the formation of plaques, which are deposits of cholesterol, fat, and other substances. These plaques can harden and narrow the arteries, a condition known as atherosclerosis. This restricts blood flow and can lead to serious cardiovascular problems, such as heart attacks and strokes.

1.1.6 Impacts on Cardiovascular Health

High cholesterol is a major risk factor for cardiovascular disease. It can lead to coronary artery disease, which is the narrowing or blockage of the coronary arteries. This can cause chest pain (angina), heart attacks, and other serious heart conditions. Managing cholesterol levels is crucial for maintaining heart health and preventing these conditions.

1.2 Risk Factors and Causes of High Cholesterol

1.2.1 Genetic Influence on Cholesterol
Genetics play a significant role in cholesterol levels. Familiar hypercholesterolemia is a genetic condition that can cause extremely high cholesterol levels and increase the risk of heart disease at a young age. Understanding your family history can help you take proactive steps in managing your cholesterol.

1.2.2 Role of Diet in Cholesterol Management
Diet is a pivotal factor in managing cholesterol. Foods high in saturated fats, trans fats, and cholesterol can increase LDL levels. Conversely, foods rich in omega-3 fatty acids, fiber, and plant sterols can help reduce LDL and increase HDL levels. A balanced diet is fundamental to maintaining healthy cholesterol levels.

1.2.3 Lifestyle and Cholesterol
Lifestyle choices significantly affect cholesterol levels. Lack of physical activity, smoking, and excessive alcohol consumption can increase LDL and lower HDL levels. Regular exercise, a balanced diet, and healthy lifestyle choices are crucial in managing cholesterol effectively.

1.2.4 Diabetes and Cholesterol
Diabetes can lead to higher levels of LDL and lower levels of HDL, as well as increased triglycerides. This combination significantly raises the risk of cardiovascular disease. Managing diabetes through diet, exercise, and medication is vital for controlling cholesterol levels.

1.2.5 Obesity and Metabolic Syndrome
Obesity and metabolic syndrome, which includes a cluster of conditions such as high blood pressure, high blood sugar, and abnormal cholesterol levels, can increase the risk of heart disease. Weight loss through a healthy diet and regular exercise can improve cholesterol levels and reduce these risks.

1.2.6 Other Medical Conditions
Certain medical conditions, such as hypothyroidism, kidney disease, and liver disease, can affect cholesterol levels. It is important to manage these conditions with the help of healthcare professionals to maintain healthy cholesterol levels.

1.3 Benefits of Lowering Cholesterol

1.3.1 Reduced Risk of Heart Attacks
Lowering cholesterol levels can significantly reduce the risk of heart attacks. By reducing LDL and increasing HDL, the buildup of plaques in the arteries is minimized, improving blood flow and reducing the risk of cardiovascular events.

1.3.2 Improved Blood Circulation
Maintaining healthy cholesterol levels helps to ensure that the arteries remain flexible and free of blockages. This improves blood circulation, delivering oxygen and nutrients efficiently throughout the body.

1.3.3 Reduction in Blood Pressure
High cholesterol can lead to high blood pressure by narrowing the arteries and making the heart work harder to pump blood. Lowering cholesterol helps to reduce blood pressure, decreasing the strain on the heart and reducing the risk of cardiovascular disease.

1.3.4 Decreased Risk of Stroke

High cholesterol can lead to the formation of blood clots, which can cause strokes if they block blood flow to the brain. Lowering cholesterol levels reduces the risk of stroke by preventing clot formation and improving overall cardiovascular health.

1.3.5 Prevention of Other Chronic Diseases

Managing cholesterol can also help prevent other chronic diseases, such as diabetes and metabolic syndrome. A healthy diet and lifestyle that keeps cholesterol levels in check can have broad health benefits, reducing the risk of multiple conditions.

1.3.6 Long-term Benefits

The long-term benefits of maintaining healthy cholesterol levels include a longer, healthier life with reduced risk of serious health issues. By adopting a heart-healthy diet and lifestyle, you can enjoy a life of vitality and well-being.

Chapter 2
Dietary Guidelines for Lowering Cholesterol

2.1 Foods to Avoid

2.1.1 Common Sources of Saturated Fats
Saturated fats are found in animal products such as red meat, butter, cheese, and whole milk. These fats can increase LDL cholesterol levels. It is important to limit these foods and opt for leaner protein sources and low-fat dairy options.

2.1.2 Effects of Trans Fats on Cholesterol
Trans fats, often found in processed foods, baked goods, and margarines, can raise LDL cholesterol and lower HDL cholesterol. Avoiding foods that contain trans fats is crucial for maintaining healthy cholesterol levels.

2.1.3 Healthier Alternatives
Replacing saturated and trans fats with healthier alternatives, such as olive oil, avocado, and nuts, can help improve cholesterol levels. These sources of healthy fats provide essential nutrients and help maintain a balanced diet.

2.1.4 How Sugars Affect Cholesterol
Refined sugars and simple carbohydrates can raise triglyceride levels and contribute to high cholesterol. These sugars are often found in sugary drinks, sweets, and processed foods. Reducing sugar intake is important for cholesterol management.

2.1.5 Avoiding Simple Carbohydrates
Simple carbohydrates are found in white bread, pasta, and many processed foods. These carbohydrates can spike blood sugar levels and contribute to high cholesterol. Opting for whole grains and complex carbohydrates can help maintain stable blood sugar and cholesterol levels.

2.1.6 Healthier Choices of Carbohydrates
Whole grains, fruits, vegetables, and legumes are excellent sources of complex carbohydrates and fiber. These foods help lower LDL cholesterol and provide essential nutrients for overall health.

2.2 Foods to Include

2.2.1 Benefits of Omega-3s
Omega-3 fatty acids, found in fatty fish, flaxseeds, and walnuts, help lower triglycerides and reduce inflammation. Including omega-3-rich foods in your diet supports heart health and lowers cholesterol levels.

2.2.2 Sources of Monounsaturated Fats
Monounsaturated fats, found in olive oil, avocados, and nuts, help improve cholesterol levels by lowering LDL and raising HDL. Incorporating these healthy fats into your diet can support overall heart health.

2.2.3 How to Incorporate These Fats into the Diet
Using olive oil for cooking, adding avocado to salads and sandwiches, and snacking on nuts are simple ways to incorporate healthy fats into your meals. These small changes can have a significant impact on cholesterol levels.

2.2.4 Benefits of Soluble Fibers
Soluble fibers, found in oats, beans, and fruits, help lower LDL cholesterol by binding to cholesterol in the digestive system and removing it from the body. Including these fibers in your diet is crucial for cholesterol management.

2.2.5 Importance of Fruits and Vegetables
Fruits and vegetables are rich in vitamins, minerals, and antioxidants that support heart health. They are also low in calories and high in fiber, making them essential components of a cholesterol-lowering diet.

2.2.6 Legumes and Cholesterol
Legumes, such as beans, lentils, and chickpeas, are excellent sources of protein and fiber. They help lower LDL cholesterol and provide a nutritious alternative to animal proteins.

2.3 The Role of Physical Activity

2.3.1 Aerobic Exercises
Aerobic exercises, such as walking, running, and cycling, are effective in raising HDL cholesterol and lowering LDL cholesterol and triglycerides. Regular aerobic exercise is crucial for maintaining heart health.

2.3.2 Endurance Exercises
Endurance exercises, like swimming and long-distance running, improve cardiovascular fitness and help manage cholesterol levels. These exercises should be incorporated into a regular fitness routine.

2.3.3 Daily Physical Activities
Incorporating physical activities into your daily routine, such as taking the stairs, gardening, or walking to work, can help improve cholesterol levels and overall health.

2.3.4 How Exercise Lowers Cholesterol
Exercise helps increase the size of LDL particles, making them less likely to form plaques in the arteries. It also boosts HDL levels and improves overall cardiovascular health.

2.3.5 Synergy Between Diet and Exercise
Combining a healthy diet with regular exercise creates a powerful synergy that enhances cholesterol management and overall well-being. This holistic approach is the foundation of a heart-healthy lifestyle.

2.3.6 Exercise Plan for Beginners
A beginner's exercise plan might include starting with 30 min. of moderate aerobic exercise, such as brisk walking, five days a week. Gradually increasing the duration and intensity can help achieve and maintain healthy cholesterol levels.

Chapter 3
Practical Cooking Tips

3.1 How to Read Nutrition Labels

3.1.1 Energy Value and Portions
Understanding the energy value and portion sizes on nutrition labels is essential for managing calorie intake and cholesterol levels. Look for the total calories and serving sizes to make informed choices.

3.1.2 Total Saturated and Trans Fats
Check the nutrition label for the amount of saturated and trans fats. These fats should be limited to reduce LDL cholesterol. Opt for foods with lower amounts of these unhealthy fats.

3.1.3 Added Sugars
Identify added sugars on the nutrition label, as they can contribute to high triglycerides and cholesterol levels. Reducing added sugars is important for maintaining a heart-healthy diet.

3.1.4 Common Names for Hidden Sugars and Fats
Hidden sugars and fats can appear under different names on ingredient lists. Learn to recognize terms like high-fructose corn syrup, hydrogenated oils, and other additives that may affect cholesterol levels.

3.1.5 Additives and Preservatives to Avoid
Certain additives and preservatives, such as sodium nitrate and artificial trans fats,

can negatively impact cholesterol levels. Opt for foods with natural ingredients and minimal processing to support heart health.

3.1.6 Healthier Alternatives
Choose products with healthier alternatives to common additives. For example, select foods with natural sweeteners like honey or maple syrup instead of high-fructose corn syrup, and opt for items with minimal preservatives.

3.2 Healthy Cooking Techniques

3.2.1 Steaming
Steaming is an excellent low-fat cooking method that preserves nutrients in vegetables, fish, and lean meats. It avoids the need for added fats, making it ideal for a cholesterol-lowering diet.

3.2.2 Grilling and Baking
Grilling and baking are healthy cooking techniques that require minimal oil and reduce the fat content of foods. These methods can bring out the natural flavors of ingredients while keeping dishes light and heart-healthy.

3.2.3 Use of Non-Stick Cookware
Non-stick cookware allows for cooking with little to no oil, reducing the fat content of meals. It is a practical tool for anyone looking to lower cholesterol through healthier cooking methods.

3.2.4 Benefits of Spices
Spices and herbs not only enhance the flavor of dishes but also offer health benefits. Many spices, such as turmeric, garlic, and ginger, have anti-inflammatory properties and can aid in cholesterol management.

3.2.5 Create Spice Mixes
Creating your own spice mixes can add a burst of flavor to meals without relying on salt or unhealthy fats. Experiment with combinations like cumin, coriander, and paprika for a heart-healthy seasoning.

3.2.6 Examples of Recipes with Spices
Incorporate spices into your meals by trying recipes like turmeric roasted cauliflower, garlic and herb chicken, or ginger-spiced vegetable stir-fry. These dishes are flavorful and support cholesterol management.

3.3 Meal Planning and Preparation

3.3.1 Importance of Planning
Meal planning is crucial for maintaining a low-cholesterol diet. It helps ensure that you have healthy ingredients on hand and reduces the temptation to opt for unhealthy options.

3.3.2 Sample Weekly Plan
A sample weekly meal plan might include oatmeal with fresh berries for breakfast, a quinoa and vegetable salad for lunch, and baked salmon with asparagus for dinner. Planning ahead makes it easier to stick to healthy eating habits.

3.3.3 Tailor the Plan to Your Personal Needs
Customize your meal plan based on your preferences and dietary needs. Include a variety of fruits, vegetables, whole grains, lean proteins, and healthy fats to support heart health.

3.3.4 Preparing Meals in Advance
Preparing meals in advance can save time and ensure that you always have healthy options available. Batch cooking and storing meals in portion-sized containers make it easy to grab and go during busy weeks.

3.3.5 Food Storage
Proper food storage is essential to maintain the freshness and nutritional value of your meals. Use airtight containers and refrigerate or freeze meals as needed to extend their shelf life.

3.3.6 Useful Tools for Meal Preparation
Invest in tools like a good set of knives, non-stick cookware, and airtight storage containers. These tools can simplify the meal preparation process and help you maintain a heart-healthy diet.

Chapter 4
Additional Resources

4.1 Glossary of Nutritional Terms

4.1.1 Common Terms
A glossary of common nutritional terms can help demystify the language of healthy eating. Terms like "LDL," "HDL," "triglycerides," and "omega-3 fatty acids" are essential to understand for managing cholesterol.

4.1.2 Detailed Explanations
Provide detailed explanations of these terms to help readers understand their significance. For example, explain how LDL cholesterol contributes to plaque buildup in arteries and how HDL cholesterol helps remove excess cholesterol.

4.1.3 Practical Examples
Include practical examples to illustrate these concepts. For instance, describe how eating foods rich in omega-3 fatty acids, like salmon and flaxseeds, can improve HDL levels and overall heart health.

4.2 Digital Tools and Resources for a Low Cholesterol Diet

4.2.1 Cholesterol Monitoring App
Recommend apps that help monitor cholesterol levels. These tools can track dietary intake, exercise, and cholesterol readings, providing valuable feedback for managing heart health.

4.2.2 Meal Planning Tools
Digital meal planning tools can simplify the process of creating and sticking to a low-cholesterol diet. These tools offer recipes, shopping lists, and customizable meal plans tailored to individual needs.

4.2.3 Forums and Online Support Communities
Encourage readers to join forums and online support communities. Connecting with others who share similar health goals can provide motivation, tips, and a sense of camaraderie.

4.3 Interactive Experiences and Bonus Material

4.3.1 Food Awareness Quiz
Create a food awareness quiz to help readers identify their knowledge gaps and learn more about cholesterol-friendly foods. This interactive element makes learning fun and engaging.

4.3.2 Healthy Shopping Checklist

Provide a healthy shopping checklist that readers can print and use during their grocery trips. This checklist should include a variety of heart-healthy foods and tips for making better choices in the store.

4.3.3 Tools to Monitor Progress

Offer tools to monitor progress, such as printable tracking sheets for cholesterol levels, exercise routines, and dietary habits. Tracking progress helps readers stay motivated and see the benefits of their efforts.

4.3.4 Step-by-Step Cooking Videos

Include links to exclusive step-by-step cooking videos. These videos can demonstrate how to prepare low-cholesterol recipes, making it easier for readers to follow along and gain confidence in the kitchen.

4.3.5 Interviews with Nutrition Experts

Feature interviews with nutrition experts who can provide insights and tips for maintaining a low-cholesterol diet. These expert perspectives add authority and depth to the content.

4.3.6 Guided Training Sessions

Offer guided training sessions for exercise routines that complement a low-cholesterol diet. These sessions can be accessed online and provide structured workouts to support heart health.

Part Two

Recipes

Breakfast

1. Avocado Toast with Tomato and Chia Seeds

Ingredients

- 2 slices of whole grain toast
- 1 ripe avocado
- 1 medium tomato, sliced
- 1 teaspoon (5 g) chia seeds
- 1 teaspoon (5 ml) fresh lemon juice
- Salt and pepper to taste
- Fresh basil leaves for garnish (optional)

Instructions

Prep Time: 10 min. **Cooking Time:** 0 min. **Total Time:** 10 min. **Difficulty:** Easy

1. Toast the slices of whole grain bread until crispy.
2. Cut the avocado in half, remove the pit, and scoop out the flesh with a spoon. Mash the avocado in a bowl with the lemon juice, salt, and pepper to taste.
3. Spread the mashed avocado evenly over the toasted bread slices.
4. Arrange the tomato slices on top of the avocado.
5. Sprinkle the chia seeds over the tomato slices.
6. Garnish with fresh basil leaves if desired.
7. Serve immediately.

Nutritional Information per Serving (1 slice)

Calories: 180; **Carbohydrates:** 20 g; **Fat:** 10 g; **Protein:** 4 g; **Saturated Fat:** 1.5 g; **Cholesterol:** 0 mg; **Sugars:** 2 g.

NOTES: You can add a sprinkle of chili powder for a spicy kick.
Substitute whole grain bread with gluten-free bread if you prefer a gluten-free version.

2. Berry Smoothie

Ingredients

- » 1 cup (150 g) mixed berries (blueberries, raspberries, strawberries)
- » 1 ripe banana
- » ½ cup (120 ml) unsweetened almond milk
- » ½ cup (120 g) low-fat Greek yogurt
- » 1 tablespoon (15 ml) maple syrup or honey (optional)
- » 1 teaspoon (5 g) chia seeds
- » Ice cubes (optional)

Instructions

Prep Time: 5 min.   **Cooking Time:** 0 min.   **Total Time:** 5 min.   **Difficulty:** Easy

1. Place all ingredients in a blender.
2. Blend until smooth and creamy.
3. Add ice cubes if you prefer a colder smoothie.
4. Pour the smoothie into a glass and serve immediately.

Nutritional Information per Serving (about 1 cup / 240 ml)

Calories: 150; **Carbohydrates:** 27 g; **Fat:** 2 g; **Protein:** 5 g; **Saturated Fat:** 0.5 g; **Cholesterol:** 0 mg; **Sugars:** 18 g.

NOTES: You can substitute almond milk with any other plant-based milk or skim milk.
For an extra flavor boost, add a splash of lemon or lime juice.

3. Oatmeal Pancakes

Ingredients

- » 1 cup (90 g) rolled oats
- » 1 cup (240 ml) unsweetened almond milk
- » 1 large egg
- » 1 ripe banana, mashed
- » 1 teaspoon (5 ml) vanilla extract
- » 1 teaspoon (5 g) baking powder
- » ½ teaspoon (2.5 g) ground cinnamon
- » A pinch of salt
- » Coconut oil or cooking spray for the pan

Instructions

Prep Time: 10 min.   **Cooking Time:** 15 min.   **Total Time:** 25 min.   **Difficulty:** Easy

1. In a blender, grind the rolled oats into a fine flour.
2. In a large bowl, mix the oat flour, almond milk, egg, mashed banana, vanilla extract, baking powder, cinnamon, and salt until well combined.
3. Heat a non-stick skillet over medium heat and lightly grease with coconut oil or cooking spray.
4. Pour about 1/4 cup of batter for each pancake into the hot skillet.
5. Cook the pancakes for 2-3 minutes on each side, or until golden brown and cooked through.
6. Serve the pancakes warm with fresh fruit, Greek yogurt, or maple syrup.

Nutritional Information per Serving (about 2 pancakes)

Calories: 150; **Carbohydrates:** 25 g; **Fat:** 4 g; **Protein:** 5 g; **Saturated Fat:** 1 g; **Cholesterol:** 55 mg; **Sugars:** 5 g.

NOTES: You can add fresh blueberries or dark chocolate chips to the batter for extra flavor.
Store leftover pancakes in the refrigerator for up to 3 days or freeze for up to 1 month.

4. Greek Yogurt with Honey and Nuts

Ingredients

- 1 cup (240 g) low-fat Greek yogurt
- 1 tablespoon (15 ml) honey
- ¼ cup (30 g) mixed nuts, chopped (walnuts, almonds, hazelnuts)
- 1 tablespoon (15 g) chia seeds or flaxseeds (optional)
- ¼ cup (40 g) fresh fruit (blueberries, strawberries, raspberries) (optional)

Instructions

Prep Time: 5 min. **Cooking Time:** 0 min. **Total Time:** 5 min. **Difficulty:** Easy

1. Spoon the Greek yogurt into a bowl.
2. Drizzle the honey over the yogurt and stir lightly to distribute the honey.
3. Sprinkle the chopped nuts and chia seeds (or flaxseeds) over the yogurt.
4. Add fresh fruit, if desired.
5. Serve immediately.

Nutritional Information per Serving (about 1 cup / 240 g)

Calories: 250; **Carbohydrates:** 25 g; **Fat:** 12 g; **Protein:** 15 g; **Saturated Fat:** 2 g; **Cholesterol:** 5 mg; **Sugars:** 20 g.

NOTES: You can substitute honey with maple syrup for a vegan version.
For extra crunch, lightly toast the nuts before adding them to the yogurt.

5. Egg White Omelette with Spinach and Feta

Ingredients

- 4 egg whites
- 1 cup (30 g) fresh spinach, chopped
- ¼ cup (30 g) crumbled feta cheese
- 1 tablespoon (15 ml) unsweetened almond milk (optional)
- 1 teaspoon (5 ml) olive oil
- Salt and pepper to taste
- Cherry tomatoes and fresh basil leaves for garnish (optional)

Instructions

Prep Time: 5 min. **Cooking Time:** 10 min. **Total Time:** 15 min. **Difficulty:** Easy

1. In a bowl, whisk the egg whites with the almond milk (if using), salt, and pepper.
2. Heat the olive oil in a non-stick skillet over medium heat.
3. Add the chopped spinach to the skillet and cook for 1-2 minutes, until wilted.
4. Pour the egg whites into the skillet and cook for 2-3 minutes, until the egg whites start to set.
5. Sprinkle the crumbled feta over half of the omelette.
6. Using a spatula, gently fold the other half of the omelette over the feta filling.
7. Cook for another 1-2 minutes, until the omelette is fully cooked and the feta is slightly melted.
8. Transfer the omelette to a plate and garnish with cherry tomatoes and fresh basil, if desired.
9. Serve immediately.

Nutritional Information per Serving

Calories: 120; **Carbohydrates:** 2 g; **Fat:** 6 g; **Protein:** 13 g; **Saturated Fat:** 2 g; **Cholesterol:** 15 mg; **Sugars:** 1 g.

NOTES: You can add other vegetables like bell peppers or mushrooms to increase the nutritional content.
For a dairy-free version, replace the feta with a vegan cheese.

6. Quinoa Porridge with Dried Fruit

Ingredients

- 1 cup (185 g) raw quinoa
- 2 cups (480 ml) unsweetened almond milk (or any other plant-based milk)
- ¼ cup (40 g) mixed dried fruit (apricots, raisins, cranberries)
- 1 tablespoon (15 ml) maple syrup or honey
- ½ teaspoon (2.5 ml) vanilla extract
- ½ teaspoon (2.5 g) ground cinnamon
- A pinch of salt
- Chopped nuts and chia seeds for garnish (optional)

Instructions

Prep Time: 5 min.   **Cooking Time:** 20 min.   **Total Time:** 25 min.   **Difficulty:** Easy

1. Rinse the quinoa under cold running water for a few minutes to remove the saponin.
2. In a medium saucepan, bring the quinoa and almond milk to a boil over medium heat.
3. Reduce the heat and let it simmer for about 15-20 minutes, or until the quinoa is cooked and has absorbed most of the liquid.
4. Add the dried fruit, maple syrup, vanilla extract, cinnamon, and a pinch of salt. Stir well.
5. Cook for another 2-3 minutes, until the dried fruit is softened and well incorporated.
6. Serve the porridge warm, garnished with chopped nuts and chia seeds if desired.

Nutritional Information per Serving (about 1 cup / 240 g)

Calories: 250; **Carbohydrates:** 45 g; **Fat:** 5 g; **Protein:** 7 g; **Saturated Fat:** 0.5 g; **Cholesterol:** 0 mg; **Sugars:** 15 g.

NOTES: You can add a splash of extra almond milk if you prefer a creamier consistency.
Store leftovers in the refrigerator for up to 3 days and reheat before serving.

7. Whole Wheat Bagel with Smoked Salmon and Avocado

Ingredients

- 1 whole wheat bagel, halved and toasted
- ½ ripe avocado, mashed
- 2 slices (about 2 oz / 60 g) smoked salmon
- ¼ cup (30 g) fresh arugula
- 1 teaspoon (5 ml) lemon juice
- Salt and pepper to taste
- Slices of tomato and red onion for garnish (optional)

Instructions

Prep Time: 10 min.   **Cooking Time:** 0 min.   **Total Time:** 10 min.   **Difficulty:** Easy

1. Toast the halved whole wheat bagel until crispy.
2. Mash the avocado in a bowl with the lemon juice, salt, and pepper to taste.
3. Spread the mashed avocado on the toasted bagel halves.
4. Layer the smoked salmon slices on top of the avocado.
5. Add fresh arugula on top of the salmon.
6. Garnish with slices of tomato and red onion, if desired.
7. Serve immediately.

Nutritional Information per Serving (1 bagel)

Calories: 350; **Carbohydrates:** 40 g; **Fat:** 15 g; **Protein:** 18 g; **Saturated Fat:** 3 g; **Cholesterol:** 30 mg; **Sugars:** 5 g.

NOTES: You can substitute the whole wheat bagel with a gluten-free bagel for a gluten-free version.
Add a sprinkle of sesame seeds or chia seeds for an extra touch of flavor and nutrients.

8. Vanilla Chia Pudding

Ingredients

- ¼ cup (40 g) chia seeds
- 1 cup (240 ml) unsweetened almond milk (or any other plant-based milk)
- 1 tablespoon (15 ml) maple syrup or honey
- 1 teaspoon (5 ml) vanilla extract
- A pinch of salt
- Fresh fruit and chopped nuts for garnish (optional)

Instructions

Prep Time: 5 min. | **Cooking Time:** 0 min. | **Chilling Time:** 4 h | **Total Time:** 4 h 5 min. | **Difficulty:** Easy

1. In a bowl, mix together the chia seeds, almond milk, maple syrup, vanilla extract, and a pinch of salt.
2. Stir well to ensure the chia seeds are evenly distributed and not clumping together.
3. Cover the bowl and refrigerate for at least 4 hours, or preferably overnight, until the pudding has thickened.
4. Before serving, stir the pudding well and divide into bowls or glasses.
5. Garnish with fresh fruit and chopped nuts if desired.

Nutritional Information per Serving (about 1/2 cup / 120 g)

Calories: 180; **Carbohydrates:** 15 g; **Fat:** 10 g; **Protein:** 4 g; **Saturated Fat:** 1 g; **Cholesterol:** 0 mg; **Sugars:** 8 g.

NOTES: You can use any plant-based milk of your choice instead of almond milk.
Add a sprinkle of cocoa powder or cinnamon for an extra flavor kick.

9. Carrot and Almond Muffins

Ingredients

- 1 cup (120 g) whole wheat flour
- 1 cup (120 g) almond flour
- 1½ teaspoons (7.5 g) baking powder
- ½ teaspoon (2.5 g) baking soda
- ½ teaspoon (2.5 g) salt
- 1½ teaspoons (7.5 g) ground cinnamon
- ¼ teaspoon (1.25 g) ground nutmeg
- 2 large eggs
- ½ cup (120 ml) unsweetened almond milk
- ¼ cup (60 ml) melted coconut oil
- ¼ cup (60 ml) maple syrup or honey
- 1 teaspoon (5 ml) vanilla extract
- 1½ cups (150 g) grated carrots
- ½ cup (60 g) chopped almonds

Instructions

Prep Time: 15 min. **Cooking Time:** 20-25 min. **Total Time:** 40 min. **Difficulty:** Easy

1. Preheat the oven to 350°F (175°C) and line a muffin tin with paper liners.
2. In a large bowl, mix together the whole wheat flour, almond flour, baking powder, baking soda, salt, cinnamon, and nutmeg.
3. In another bowl, whisk together the eggs, almond milk, coconut oil, maple syrup, and vanilla extract until smooth.
4. Add the wet ingredients to the dry ingredients and mix gently until just combined.
5. Fold in the grated carrots and chopped almonds.
6. Divide the batter evenly among the muffin cups, filling them about 2/3 full.
7. Bake for 20-25 minutes, or until a toothpick inserted into the center comes out clean.
8. Let the muffins cool in the tin for 5 minutes, then transfer them to a wire rack to cool completely.

Nutritional Information per Muffin

Calories: 180; **Carbohydrates:** 20 g; **Fat:** 10 g; **Protein:** 5 g; **Saturated Fat:** 3 g; **Cholesterol:** 30 mg; **Sugars:** 8 g.

NOTES: You can add a handful of raisins or chopped walnuts for extra flavor and nutrients.
Store the muffins in an airtight container for up to 3 days or freeze for up to 1 month.

10. Whole Wheat Bread Toast with Almond Butter and Banana

Ingredients

- 2 slices of whole wheat bread
- 2 tablespoons (30 g) natural almond butter
- 1 banana, sliced
- 1 teaspoon (5 g) chia seeds (optional)
- A pinch of ground cinnamon (optional)
- Honey or maple syrup for drizzling (optional)

Instructions

Prep Time: 5 min. **Cooking Time:** 5 min. **Total Time:** 10 min. **Difficulty:** Easy

1. Toast the slices of whole wheat bread until golden and crispy.
2. Spread the almond butter evenly on the toasted bread slices.
3. Arrange the banana slices on top of the almond butter.
4. Sprinkle the chia seeds and a pinch of cinnamon over the banana slices, if desired.
5. Drizzle with honey or maple syrup for extra sweetness, if desired.
6. Serve immediately.

Nutritional Information per Serving (1 toast)

Calories: 250; **Carbohydrates:** 30 g; **Fat:** 12 g; **Protein:** 7 g; **Saturated Fat:** 1 g; **Cholesterol:** 0 mg; **Sugars:** 10 g.

NOTES: You can substitute almond butter with peanut butter or cashew butter.

Add strawberry slices or blueberries for an extra touch of freshness and color.

11. Green Detox Smoothie

Ingredients

- 1 cup (30 g) fresh spinach
- ½ cup (120 ml) unsweetened almond milk (or any other plant-based milk)
- 1 ripe banana
- ½ cup (75 g) fresh pineapple chunks
- ½ cucumber, peeled and chopped
- 1 tablespoon (15 ml) fresh lemon juice
- 1 teaspoon (5 g) chia seeds
- 1 teaspoon (5 g) grated fresh ginger (optional)
- Ice cubes (optional)

Instructions

Prep Time: 5 min. **Cooking Time:** 0 min. **Total Time:** 5 min. **Difficulty:** Easy

1. Place all ingredients in a blender.
2. Blend until smooth and creamy.
3. Add ice cubes if you prefer a colder smoothie.
4. Pour the smoothie into a glass and serve immediately.

Nutritional Information per Serving (about 1 cup / 240 ml)

Calories: 120; **Carbohydrates:** 26 g; **Fat:** 2 g; **Protein:** 2 g; **Saturated Fat:** 0.5 g; **Cholesterol:** 0 mg; **Sugars:** 14 g.

NOTES: You can add a handful of kale to increase the nutrient content.
For extra sweetness, add a teaspoon of honey or maple syrup.

12. Yogurt Parfait with Granola and Fruit

Ingredients

- 1 cup (240 g) low-fat Greek yogurt
- ½ cup (60 g) low-sugar granola
- ½ cup (75 g) mixed fresh fruit (blueberries, strawberries, raspberries, bananas)
- 1 tablespoon (15 ml) honey or maple syrup (optional)
- 1 tablespoon (10 g) chia seeds or flaxseeds (optional)
- Fresh mint leaves for garnish (optional)

Instructions

Prep Time: 5 min. **Cooking Time:** 0 min. **Total Time:** 5 min. **Difficulty:** Easy

1. Start with a layer of Greek yogurt at the bottom of a glass or parfait cup.
2. Add a layer of granola, followed by a layer of fresh fruit.
3. Repeat the layers until the glass is filled, ending with a layer of fruit.
4. Drizzle with honey or maple syrup if desired.
5. Sprinkle chia seeds or flaxseeds on top.
6. Garnish with fresh mint leaves.
7. Serve immediately or refrigerate until ready to serve.

Nutritional Information per Serving (about 1 cup / 240 g)

Calories: 250; **Carbohydrates:** 38 g; **Fat:** 5 g; **Protein:** 14 g; **Saturated Fat:** 1 g; **Cholesterol:** 5 mg; **Sugars:** 18 g.

NOTES: You can use any combination of seasonal fruit to vary the flavor.
For a vegan version, use soy or coconut yogurt and maple syrup instead of honey.

13. Whole Wheat Waffles with Fresh Fruit

Ingredients

- 1½ cups (180 g) whole wheat flour
- 2 tablespoons (25 g) brown sugar
- 1½ teaspoons (7.5 g) baking powder
- ½ teaspoon (2.5 g) baking soda
- ½ teaspoon (2.5 g) salt
- 1¾ cups (420 ml) unsweetened almond milk (or any other plant-based milk)
- ¼ cup (60 ml) melted coconut oil or sunflower oil
- 2 large eggs
- 1 teaspoon (5 ml) vanilla extract
- Fresh fruit of your choice (strawberries, blueberries, bananas)
- Maple syrup or honey for serving (optional)

Instructions

Prep Time: 10 min. **Cooking Time:** 20 min. **Total Time:** 30 min. **Difficulty:** Easy

1. Preheat your waffle iron according to the manufacturer's instructions.
2. In a large bowl, whisk together the whole wheat flour, brown sugar, baking powder, baking soda, and salt.
3. In another bowl, whisk together the almond milk, melted coconut oil, eggs, and vanilla extract until smooth.
4. Pour the wet ingredients into the dry ingredients and mix gently until just combined. Do not overmix.
5. Pour about 1/2 cup of batter into the preheated waffle iron and cook until the waffles are golden brown and crispy.
6. Repeat with the remaining batter.
7. Serve the waffles warm with fresh fruit and, if desired, a drizzle of maple syrup or honey.

Nutritional Information per Serving (about 1 waffle)

Calories: 220; **Carbohydrates:** 30 g; **Fat:** 9 g; **Protein:** 6 g; **Saturated Fat:** 3 g; **Cholesterol:** 55 mg; **Sugars:** 7 g.

NOTES: You can add a handful of chopped nuts or chia seeds to the batter for extra flavor and nutrients.
Store leftover waffles in the refrigerator for up to 3 days or freeze for up to 1 month. Reheat before serving.

14. Tofu Scramble with Vegetables

Ingredients
- 1 block (14 oz / 400 g) extra-firm tofu, drained and crumbled
- 1 tablespoon (15 ml) olive oil
- 1 small onion, chopped
- 1 red bell pepper, chopped
- 1 medium zucchini, chopped
- 1 cup (30 g) fresh spinach
- ½ teaspoon (2.5 g) ground turmeric
- ½ teaspoon (2.5 g) ground cumin
- ¼ teaspoon (1.25 g) paprika
- Salt and pepper to taste
- 1 tablespoon (15 ml) low-sodium soy sauce
- Fresh herbs (parsley or cilantro) for garnish (optional)

Instructions

Prep Time: 10 min. **Cooking Time:** 15 min. **Total Time:** 25 min. **Difficulty:** Easy

1. Heat the olive oil in a large skillet over medium heat.
2. Add the onion and cook for 2-3 minutes, until it becomes translucent.
3. Add the red bell pepper and zucchini, and cook for another 5-7 minutes, until the vegetables are tender.
4. Add the crumbled tofu to the skillet and stir well.
5. Add the turmeric, cumin, paprika, salt, and pepper. Stir well to combine.
6. Add the fresh spinach and soy sauce, and cook for another 2-3 minutes, until the spinach is wilted and the tofu is heated through.
7. Serve hot, garnished with fresh herbs if desired.

Nutritional Information per Serving (about 1 cup / 240 g)
Calories: 180; **Carbohydrates:** 10 g; **Fat:** 12 g; **Protein:** 14 g; **Saturated Fat:** 1.5 g; **Cholesterol:** 0 mg; **Sugars:** 3 g.

NOTES: You can add other vegetables like mushrooms, tomatoes, or carrots to increase the nutritional content. Serve with a slice of whole wheat toast for a complete and balanced meal.

15. Overnight Oats with Chia Seeds and Fruit

Ingredients

- ½ cup (45 g) rolled oats
- 1 cup (240 ml) unsweetened almond milk (or any other plant-based milk)
- 1 tablespoon (15 g) chia seeds
- 1 tablespoon (15 ml) maple syrup or honey (optional)
- ½ teaspoon (2.5 ml) vanilla extract
- ½ cup (75 g) fresh fruit (strawberries, blueberries, bananas, raspberries)
- 1 tablespoon (15 g) chopped nuts (optional)

Instructions

Prep Time: 5 min. | **Cooking Time:** 0 min. | **Chilling Time:** 4 h or overnight | **Total Time:** 4 h 5 min. | **Difficulty:** Easy

1. In a jar or container with a lid, combine the rolled oats, almond milk, chia seeds, maple syrup, and vanilla extract.
2. Stir well to ensure all ingredients are well combined.
3. Cover the container and refrigerate for at least 4 hours, or overnight.
4. When ready to serve, stir the overnight oats well.
5. Add fresh fruit and chopped nuts, if desired.
6. Serve cold.

Nutritional Information per Serving (about 1 cup / 240 g)

Calories: 250; **Carbohydrates:** 40 g; **Fat:** 8 g; **Protein:** 6 g; **Saturated Fat:** 1 g; **Cholesterol:** 0 mg; **Sugars:** 12 g.

NOTES: You can substitute almond milk with any other plant-based milk or skim milk.
Add a sprinkle of cinnamon or cocoa powder for extra flavor.

Lunch Recipes

1. Quinoa and Vegetable Salad

Description
This quinoa and vegetable salad is perfect for health-conscious individuals looking for a light, protein-rich, and low-fat meal. Easy to prepare and full of fresh flavors, it's ideal for a nutritious lunch or light dinner.

Ingredients
- 1 cup (185 g) raw quinoa
- 2 cups (480 ml) water
- 1 cup (150 g) cherry tomatoes, halved
- 1 medium cucumber, diced
- 1 red bell pepper, diced
- 1 cup (150 g) corn (fresh or frozen)
- ¼ cup (30 g) finely chopped red onion
- ¼ cup (15 g) fresh parsley, chopped
- ¼ cup (60 ml) extra virgin olive oil
- 2 tablespoons (30 ml) fresh lemon juice
- 1 teaspoon (5 ml) apple cider vinegar
- Salt and pepper to taste
- Fresh mint leaves for garnish (optional)

Instructions

Prep Time: 15 min. **Cooking Time:** 15 min. **Total Time:** 30 min. **Difficulty:** Easy

1. Rinse the quinoa under cold running water. In a medium saucepan, bring the water to a boil and add the quinoa. Reduce the heat, cover, and simmer for about 15 minutes, or until the quinoa is cooked and has absorbed all the water. Let cool.
2. In a large bowl, combine the cooked quinoa, cherry tomatoes, cucumber, red bell pepper, corn, red onion, and parsley.
3. In a small bowl, whisk together the olive oil, lemon juice, apple cider vinegar, salt, and pepper.
4. Pour the dressing over the quinoa salad and mix well to combine.
5. Garnish with fresh mint leaves, if desired.
6. Serve immediately or refrigerate until ready to serve.

Nutritional Information per Serving (about 1 cup / 240 g)
Calories: 220; **Carbohydrates:** 28 g; **Fat:** 10 g; **Protein:** 5 g; **Saturated Fat:** 1.5 g; **Cholesterol:** 0 mg; **Sugars:** 3 g.

NOTES: You can add other vegetables like zucchini, carrots, or avocado for varied flavor and texture.
Store the salad in an airtight container in the refrigerator for up to 3 days.

2. Grilled Chicken Wrap

Description

This grilled chicken wrap is perfect for health-conscious individuals looking for a light, protein-rich, and low-fat meal. Easy to prepare and delicious, it's ideal for a nutritious lunch or dinner.

Ingredients

- 2 boneless, skinless chicken breasts
- 1 tablespoon (15 ml) olive oil
- Salt and pepper to taste
- 1 teaspoon (5 g) paprika
- 1 teaspoon (5 g) garlic powder
- 1 teaspoon (5 g) onion powder
- 4 whole wheat tortillas
- 1 cup (240 g) romaine lettuce, chopped
- 1 large tomato, sliced
- ½ cucumber, sliced
- ¼ cup (60 g) low-fat hummus
- ¼ cup (60 g) low-fat Greek yogurt
- Lemon juice to taste

Instructions

Prep Time: 10 min. | **Cooking Time:** 15 min. | **Total Time:** 25 min. | **Difficulty:** Easy

1. Preheat the grill to medium-high heat.
2. Brush the chicken breasts with olive oil and season with salt, pepper, paprika, garlic powder, and onion powder.
3. Grill the chicken for about 6-7 minutes per side, or until fully cooked. Let cool slightly, then slice into thin strips.
4. Warm the whole wheat tortillas on the grill or in a skillet.
5. Spread a layer of hummus and Greek yogurt on each tortilla.
6. Add the chopped lettuce, tomato slices, cucumber slices, and grilled chicken strips.
7. Add a squeeze of lemon juice to taste.
8. Wrap the tortillas to form wraps, cut them in half, and serve immediately.

Nutritional Information per Serving (1 wrap)

Calories: 300; **Carbohydrates:** 30 g; **Fat:** 10 g; **Protein:** 25 g; **Saturated Fat:** 2 g; **Cholesterol:** 50 mg; **Sugars:** 3 g.

NOTES: You can add other vegetables like bell peppers, carrots, or avocado for varied flavor and texture.
Store leftover wraps in an airtight container in the refrigerator for up to 2 days.

3. Lentil Soup

Description

This lentil soup is perfect for health-conscious individuals looking for a protein-rich, fiber-filled, and low-fat meal. Easy to prepare, delicious, and nutritious, it's ideal for a comforting lunch or dinner.

Ingredients

- 1 cup (200 g) dried lentils, rinsed and drained
- 1 tablespoon (15 ml) olive oil
- 1 medium onion, chopped
- 2 carrots, peeled and diced
- 2 celery stalks, diced
- 3 garlic cloves, minced
- 1 large tomato, diced (or 1 can 14 oz / 400 g diced tomatoes, drained)
- 6 cups (1.4 L) low-sodium vegetable broth
- 1 teaspoon (5 g) ground cumin
- 1 teaspoon (5 g) ground coriander
- ½ teaspoon (2.5 g) ground turmeric
- 1 bay leaf
- Salt and pepper to taste
- ¼ cup (15 g) fresh parsley, chopped (optional)
- Fresh lemon juice to taste

Instructions

Prep Time: 10 min. **Cooking Time:** 35-40 min. **Total Time:** 45-50 min. **Difficulty:** Easy

1. In a large pot, heat the olive oil over medium heat. Add the onion, carrots, and celery. Cook for 5-7 minutes, until the vegetables are tender.
2. Add the minced garlic and cook for 1 minute, until fragrant.
3. Add the diced tomatoes, lentils, vegetable broth, cumin, coriander, turmeric, and bay leaf. Bring to a boil.
4. Reduce the heat, cover, and simmer for 30-35 minutes, until the lentils are tender.
5. Remove the bay leaf and season with salt and pepper to taste.
6. Serve hot, garnished with fresh parsley and a squeeze of lemon juice.

Nutritional Information per Serving (about 1 cup / 240 g)

Calories: 200; **Carbohydrates:** 30 g; **Fat:** 5 g; **Protein:** 12 g; **Saturated Fat:** 0.5 g; **Cholesterol:** 0 mg; **Sugars:** 4 g.

NOTES: You can add other vegetables like zucchini, spinach, or bell peppers to vary the flavor and increase the nutritional content.
Store leftover soup in an airtight container in the refrigerator for up to 5 days, or freeze for up to 3 months.

4. Chickpea and Spinach Salad

Description

This chickpea and spinach salad is perfect for health-conscious individuals looking for a light, protein-rich, and low-fat meal. Easy to prepare and delicious, it's ideal for a nutritious lunch or dinner.

Ingredients

- 1 can (15 oz / 425 g) chickpeas, drained and rinsed
- 4 cups (120 g) fresh spinach
- 1 red bell pepper, diced
- 1 medium cucumber, diced
- ¼ cup (30 g) finely chopped red onion
- ¼ cup (15 g) fresh parsley, chopped
- ¼ cup (60 ml) extra virgin olive oil
- 2 tablespoons (30 ml) fresh lemon juice
- 1 teaspoon (5 ml) apple cider vinegar
- 1 teaspoon (5 g) Dijon mustard
- 1 garlic clove, minced
- Salt and pepper to taste

Instructions

Prep Time: 15 min. **Cooking Time:** 0 min. **Total Time:** 15 min. **Difficulty:** Easy

1. In a large bowl, combine the chickpeas, spinach, red bell pepper, cucumber, red onion, and parsley.
2. In a small bowl, whisk together the olive oil, lemon juice, apple cider vinegar, Dijon mustard, minced garlic, salt, and pepper.
3. Pour the dressing over the salad and toss well to combine.
4. Serve immediately or refrigerate until ready to serve.

Nutritional Information per Serving (about 1 cup / 240 g)

Calories: 200; **Carbohydrates:** 18 g; **Fat:** 12 g; **Protein:** 6 g; **Saturated Fat:** 1.5 g; **Cholesterol:** 0 mg; **Sugars:** 3 g.

NOTES: You can add other vegetables like cherry tomatoes, carrots, or avocado for varied flavor and texture. Store the salad in an airtight container in the refrigerator for up to 3 days.

5. Fish Tacos

Description

These fish tacos are perfect for health-conscious individuals looking for a light, protein-rich, and low-fat meal. Easy to prepare and delicious, they are ideal for a nutritious lunch or dinner.

Ingredients

- 1 lb (450 g) white fish fillets (such as tilapia, cod, or halibut)
- 1 tablespoon (15 ml) olive oil
- 1 teaspoon (5 g) paprika
- 1 teaspoon (5 g) ground cumin
- ½ teaspoon (2.5 g) garlic powder
- ½ teaspoon (2.5 g) onion powder
- ½ teaspoon (2.5 g) chili powder
- Salt and pepper to taste
- 8 whole wheat or corn tortillas
- 2 cups (150 g) shredded red cabbage
- 1 cup (150 g) cherry tomatoes, halved
- 1 avocado, sliced
- ¼ cup (60 g) low-fat Greek yogurt
- 2 tablespoons (30 ml) fresh lime juice
- Fresh cilantro leaves for garnish

Instructions

Prep Time: 10 min. **Cooking Time:** 10 min. **Total Time:** 20 min. **Difficulty:** Easy

1. Preheat the oven to 375°F (190°C) or heat a grill to medium-high heat.
2. Brush the fish fillets with olive oil and season with paprika, cumin, garlic powder, onion powder, chili powder, salt, and pepper.
3. Cook the fish in the oven or on the grill for 5-7 minutes per side, or until cooked through and easily flaked with a fork.
4. Lightly warm the whole wheat or corn tortillas.
5. In a bowl, mix the Greek yogurt with the lime juice.
6. Assemble the tacos by placing the cooked fish in the center of each tortilla. Add shredded red cabbage, cherry tomatoes, avocado slices, and a dollop of lime yogurt.
7. Garnish with fresh cilantro leaves.
8. Serve immediately.

Nutritional Information per Serving (2 tacos)

Calories: 350; **Carbohydrates:** 40 g; **Fat:** 12 g; **Protein:** 22 g; **Saturated Fat:** 2 g; **Cholesterol:** 45 mg; **Sugars:** 3 g.

NOTES: You can add hot sauce or mango salsa for an extra flavor kick.
Store the ingredients separately in the refrigerator for up to 2 days and assemble the tacos just before serving.

6. Grilled Chicken with Roasted Vegetables

Description

This grilled chicken with roasted vegetables dish is perfect for health-conscious individuals looking for a protein-rich and low-fat meal. Easy to prepare and delicious, it's ideal for a nutritious lunch or dinner.

Ingredients

For the Chicken:
- 2 boneless, skinless chicken breasts
- 1 tablespoon (15 ml) olive oil
- 1 teaspoon (5 g) paprika
- 1 teaspoon (5 g) garlic powder
- 1 teaspoon (5 g) onion powder
- ½ teaspoon (2.5 g) ground cumin
- Salt and pepper to taste
- Juice of half a lemon

For the Roasted Vegetables:
- 1 red bell pepper, sliced
- 1 yellow bell pepper, sliced
- 1 medium zucchini, sliced into rounds
- 1 red onion, sliced
- 1 cup (150 g) cherry tomatoes
- 2 tablespoons (30 ml) olive oil
- 1 teaspoon (5 g) Italian seasoning (basil, oregano, thyme)
- Salt and pepper to taste

Instructions

Prep Time: 15 min. **Cooking Time:** 30 min. **Total Time:** 45 min. **Difficulty:** Easy

For the Chicken:
1. Preheat the grill to medium-high heat.
2. In a bowl, mix the olive oil, paprika, garlic powder, onion powder, cumin, salt, pepper, and lemon juice.
3. Brush the chicken breasts with the marinade.
4. Grill the chicken for 6-7 minutes per side, or until fully cooked.

For the Roasted Vegetables:
1. Preheat the oven to 400°F (200°C).
2. In a large bowl, toss the vegetables with olive oil, Italian seasoning, salt, and pepper.
3. Spread the vegetables on a baking sheet lined with parchment paper.
4. Roast for 20-25 min., or until the vegetables are tender and slightly golden.
5. Serve the grilled chicken with the roasted vegetables. You can garnish with fresh herbs if desired.

Nutritional Information per Serving

Calories: 350; **Carbohydrates:** 20 g; **Fat:** 15 g; **Protein:** 30 g; **Saturated Fat:** 2.5 g; **Cholesterol:** 75 mg; **Sugars:** 8 g.

NOTES: You can add other vegetables like carrots, sweet potatoes, or mushrooms for varied flavor and texture. Store leftovers in an airtight container in the refrigerator for up to 3 days.

7. Spelt and Vegetable Salad

Description
This spelt and vegetable salad is perfect for health-conscious individuals looking for a light, protein-rich, and low-fat meal. Easy to prepare and delicious, it's ideal for a nutritious lunch or dinner.

Ingredients
- 1 cup (200 g) spelt
- 2 cups (480 ml) water or low-sodium vegetable broth
- 1 cup (150 g) cherry tomatoes, halved
- 1 medium cucumber, diced
- 1 red bell pepper, diced
- 1 cup (150 g) corn (fresh or frozen)
- ¼ cup (30 g) finely chopped red onion
- ¼ cup (15 g) fresh parsley, chopped
- ¼ cup (60 ml) extra virgin olive oil
- 2 tablespoons (30 ml) fresh lemon juice
- 1 teaspoon (5 ml) apple cider vinegar
- 1 teaspoon (5 g) Dijon mustard
- 1 garlic clove, minced
- Salt and pepper to taste

Instructions

Prep Time: 15 min.   **Cooking Time:** 30 min.   **Total Time:** 45 min.   **Difficulty:** Easy

1. Rinse the spelt under cold running water. In a medium saucepan, bring the water or vegetable broth to a boil. Add the spelt, reduce the heat, cover, and simmer for about 30 minutes, or until the spelt is tender. Drain and let cool.
2. In a large bowl, combine the cooked spelt, cherry tomatoes, cucumber, red bell pepper, corn, red onion, and parsley.
3. In a small bowl, whisk together the olive oil, lemon juice, apple cider vinegar, Dijon mustard, minced garlic, salt, and pepper.
4. Pour the dressing over the salad and toss well to combine.
5. Serve immediately or refrigerate until ready to serve.

Nutritional Information per Serving (about 1 cup / 240 g)
Calories: 250; **Carbohydrates:** 35 g; **Fat:** 10 g; **Protein:** 6 g; **Saturated Fat:** 1.5 g; **Cholesterol:** 0 mg; **Sugars:** 4 g.

NOTES: You can add other vegetables like zucchini, carrots, or avocado for varied flavor and texture.
Store the salad in an airtight container in the refrigerator for up to 3 days.

8. Hummus & Vegetable Wrap

Description
This hummus and vegetable wrap is perfect for health-conscious individuals looking for a light, fiber-rich, and low-fat meal. Easy to prepare and delicious, it's ideal for a nutritious lunch or snack.

Ingredients
- 4 whole wheat tortillas
- 1 cup (240 g) low-fat hummus
- 1 cup (120 g) shredded carrots
- 1 medium cucumber, sliced into thin strips
- 1 red bell pepper, sliced into thin strips
- 1 cup (30 g) fresh spinach
- 1 avocado, sliced
- ¼ cup (30 g) finely chopped red onion
- Fresh lemon juice to taste
- Salt and pepper to taste

Instructions

Prep Time: 10 min. | **Cooking Time:** 0 min. | **Total Time:** 10 min. | **Difficulty:** Easy

1. Spread a generous amount of hummus on each whole wheat tortilla.
2. Evenly distribute the shredded carrots, cucumber, red bell pepper, spinach, avocado, and red onion over the hummus.
3. Squeeze some fresh lemon juice over the vegetables and season with salt and pepper to taste.
4. Roll up each tortilla to form a wrap.
5. Cut in half and serve immediately.

Nutritional Information per Serving (1 wrap)
Calories: 250; **Carbohydrates:** 35 g; **Fat:** 10 g; **Protein:** 6 g; **Saturated Fat:** 1.5 g; **Cholesterol:** 0 mg; **Sugars:** 5 g.

NOTES: You can add other vegetables like tomatoes, zucchini, or mushrooms for varied flavor and texture. Store leftover wraps in an airtight container in the refrigerator for up to 2 days.

9. Brown Rice with Vegetable Curry

Description
This brown rice with vegetable curry is perfect for health-conscious individuals looking for a fiber-rich, plant-based protein meal that's low in fat. Easy to prepare and delicious, it's ideal for a nutritious lunch or dinner.

Ingredients

For the Brown Rice:
- 1 cup (200 g) brown rice
- 2½ cups (600 ml) water
- A pinch of salt

For the Vegetable Curry:
- 1 tablespoon (15 ml) coconut oil or olive oil
- 1 medium onion, chopped
- 3 garlic cloves, minced
- 1 tablespoon (15 g) grated fresh ginger
- 1 red bell pepper, diced
- 2 carrots, sliced
- 1 medium zucchini, diced
- 1 cup (150 g) frozen peas
- 1 can (14 oz / 400 ml) light coconut milk
- 1 can (14 oz / 400 g) diced tomatoes
- 2 tablespoons (30 g) red curry paste (or to taste)
- 1 teaspoon (5 g) ground turmeric
- 1 teaspoon (5 g) ground cumin
- 1 teaspoon (5 g) ground coriander
- Salt and pepper to taste
- Juice of 1 lime
- Fresh cilantro leaves for garnish

Instructions

For the Brown Rice:
1. Rinse the brown rice under cold running water.
2. In a medium saucepan, bring the water to a boil with a pinch of salt.
3. Add the rice, reduce the heat, cover, and simmer for about 40-45 minutes, or until the rice is tender and has absorbed all the water.
4. Remove from heat and let it sit, covered, for 10 minutes, then fluff with a fork.

For the Vegetable Curry:
1. In a large skillet, heat the coconut oil over medium heat.
2. Add the onion, garlic, and ginger and cook for 5 min., until the onion is translucent.
3. Add the bell pepper, carrots, and zucchini and cook for another 5 min..
4. Add the peas, coconut milk, diced tomatoes, curry paste, turmeric, cumin, coriander, salt, and pepper.
5. Bring to a boil, then reduce the heat and simmer for 15-20 min., until the vegetables are tender and the curry has thickened.
6. Stir in the lime juice.

Assembly:
1. Serve the hot vegetable curry over the cooked brown rice.
2. Garnish with fresh cilantro leaves.

Nutritional Information per Serving (about 1 cup rice and 1 cup curry)
Calories: 350; **Carbohydrates:** 55 g; **Fat:** 12 g; **Protein:** 7 g; **Saturated Fat:** 5 g; **Cholesterol:** 0 mg; **Sugars:** 8 g.

NOTES: You can add other vegetables like spinach, broccoli, or green beans for varied flavor and increased nutritional content.
Store leftovers in an airtight container in the refrigerator for up to 3 days.

10. Baked Salmon with Asparagus

Description

This baked salmon with asparagus dish is perfect for health-conscious individuals looking for a protein-rich meal with healthy fats but low in saturated fats. Easy to prepare and delicious, it's ideal for a nutritious lunch or dinner.

Ingredients

- 4 salmon fillets (about 4 oz / 115 g each)
- 1 bunch of asparagus, trimmed
- 2 tablespoons (30 ml) extra virgin olive oil
- 2 garlic cloves, minced
- Juice of 1 lemon
- Zest of 1 lemon
- 1 teaspoon (5 g) fresh thyme, chopped (or ½ teaspoon dried thyme)
- Salt and pepper to taste
- Lemon slices for garnish (optional)

Instructions

Prep Time: 10 min. **Cooking Time:** 20 min. **Total Time:** 30 min. **Difficulty:** Easy

1. Preheat the oven to 400°F (200°C).
2. Arrange the salmon fillets on a baking sheet lined with parchment paper.
3. Arrange the asparagus spears next to the salmon fillets on the baking sheet.
4. In a small bowl, mix together the olive oil, minced garlic, lemon juice, lemon zest, and thyme.
5. Brush the olive oil mixture over the salmon fillets and asparagus. Season with salt and pepper to taste.
6. Bake in the oven for 15-20 minutes, or until the salmon is cooked through and flakes easily with a fork, and the asparagus is tender.
7. Serve warm, garnished with lemon slices if desired.

Nutritional Information per Serving (1 salmon fillet and a portion of asparagus)

Calories: 350; **Carbohydrates:** 5 g; **Fat:** 25 g; **Protein:** 28 g; **Saturated Fat:** 4 g; **Cholesterol:** 70 mg; **Sugars:** 2 g.

NOTES: You can add other vegetables like cherry tomatoes or sweet potatoes for varied flavor and texture. Store leftovers in an airtight container in the refrigerator for up to 3 days.

11. Arugula and Avocado Salad

Description
This arugula and avocado salad is perfect for health-conscious individuals looking for a light, nutrient-rich, and low-fat meal. Easy to prepare and delicious, it's ideal for a nutritious lunch or light dinner.

Ingredients
- 4 cups (120 g) fresh arugula
- 1 ripe avocado, sliced
- 1 cup (150 g) cherry tomatoes, halved
- 1 medium cucumber, sliced into rounds
- ¼ cup (30 g) thinly sliced red onion
- 2 tablespoons (30 ml) extra virgin olive oil
- 1 tablespoon (15 ml) fresh lemon juice
- 1 teaspoon (5 ml) balsamic vinegar
- Salt and pepper to taste
- ¼ cup (30 g) toasted nuts or pumpkin seeds (optional)

Instructions

Prep Time: 10 min.   **Cooking Time:** 0 min.   **Total Time:** 10 min.   **Difficulty:** Easy

1. In a large bowl, combine the arugula, avocado, cherry tomatoes, cucumber, and red onion.
2. In a small bowl, whisk together the olive oil, lemon juice, balsamic vinegar, salt, and pepper.
3. Pour the dressing over the salad and gently toss to combine.
4. Garnish with toasted nuts or pumpkin seeds, if desired.
5. Serve immediately.

Nutritional Information per Serving (about 1 cup / 240 g)
Calories: 220; **Carbohydrates:** 12 g; **Fat:** 18 g; **Protein:** 3 g; **Saturated Fat:** 2.5 g; **Cholesterol:** 0 mg; **Sugars:** 3 g.

NOTES: You can add other vegetables like bell peppers, carrots, or radishes for varied flavor and texture.
Store the salad without dressing in an airtight container in the refrigerator for up to 2 days and add the dressing just before serving.

12. Vegetable Minestrone

Description

This vegetable minestrone is perfect for health-conscious individuals looking for a nutrient-rich, low-fat meal. Easy to prepare and delicious, it's ideal for a light and nutritious lunch or dinner.

Ingredients

- 2 tablespoons (30 ml) extra virgin olive oil
- 1 medium onion, chopped
- 2 carrots, peeled and diced
- 2 celery stalks, diced
- 3 garlic cloves, minced
- 1 medium zucchini, diced
- 1 red bell pepper, diced
- 1 cup (150 g) green beans, cut into pieces
- 1 can (14 oz / 400 g) diced tomatoes
- 6 cups (1.4 L) low-sodium vegetable broth
- 1 can (15 oz / 425 g) cannellini beans, drained and rinsed
- 1 cup (150 g) frozen peas
- 1 cup (150 g) chopped kale
- 1 teaspoon (5 g) dried thyme
- 1 teaspoon (5 g) dried oregano
- 1 bay leaf
- Salt and pepper to taste
- ½ cup (50 g) whole wheat pasta (optional)
- Grated Parmesan cheese for serving (optional)
- Fresh basil leaves for garnish (optional)

Instructions

Prep Time: 15 min. **Cooking Time:** 30 min. **Total Time:** 45 min. **Difficulty:** Easy

1. In a large pot, heat the olive oil over medium heat.
2. Add the onion, carrots, and celery. Cook for 5-7 minutes, until the vegetables are tender.
3. Add the garlic and cook for 1 minute, until fragrant.
4. Add the zucchini, red bell pepper, and green beans. Cook for another 5 minutes.
5. Add the diced tomatoes, vegetable broth, cannellini beans, peas, kale, thyme, oregano, and bay leaf. Bring to a boil.
6. Reduce the heat and simmer for 15-20 minutes, until the vegetables are tender.
7. If using pasta, add it during the last 10 minutes of cooking.
8. Remove the bay leaf and season with salt and pepper to taste.
9. Serve hot, with grated Parmesan cheese and fresh basil leaves, if desired.

Nutritional Information per Serving (about 1 cup / 240 g)

Calories: 200; **Carbohydrates:** 30 g; **Fat:** 6 g; **Protein:** 6 g; **Saturated Fat:** 1 g; **Cholesterol:** 0 mg; **Sugars:** 7 g.

NOTES: You can add other vegetables like spinach, broccoli, or kale for varied flavor and increased nutritional content.
Store leftover minestrone in an airtight container in the refrigerator for up to 5 days, or freeze for up to 3 months.

13. Couscous and Chickpea Salad

Description

This couscous and chickpea salad is perfect for health-conscious individuals looking for a light, protein-rich, and low-fat meal. Easy to prepare and delicious, it's ideal for a nutritious lunch or dinner.

Ingredients

- 1 cup (170 g) whole wheat couscous
- 1¼ cups (300 ml) water or low-sodium vegetable broth
- 1 can (15 oz / 425 g) chickpeas, drained and rinsed
- 1 cup (150 g) cherry tomatoes, halved
- 1 medium cucumber, diced
- 1 red bell pepper, diced
- ¼ cup (30 g) finely chopped red onion
- ¼ cup (15 g) fresh parsley, chopped
- ¼ cup (60 ml) extra virgin olive oil
- 2 tablespoons (30 ml) fresh lemon juice
- 1 teaspoon (5 ml) apple cider vinegar
- 1 teaspoon (5 g) Dijon mustard
- Salt and pepper to taste
- Fresh mint leaves for garnish (optional)

Instructions

Prep Time: 15 min. | **Cooking Time:** 5 min. | **Total Time:** 20 min. | **Difficulty:** Easy

1. Bring the water or vegetable broth to a boil in a medium saucepan. Add the couscous, cover, and remove from heat. Let sit for 5 minutes, then fluff with a fork.
2. In a large bowl, combine the cooked couscous, chickpeas, cherry tomatoes, cucumber, red bell pepper, red onion, and parsley.
3. In a small bowl, whisk together the olive oil, lemon juice, apple cider vinegar, Dijon mustard, salt, and pepper.
4. Pour the dressing over the salad and toss well to combine.
5. Garnish with fresh mint leaves, if desired.
6. Serve immediately or refrigerate until ready to serve.

Nutritional Information per Serving (about 1 cup / 240 g)

Calories: 220; **Carbohydrates:** 30 g; **Fat:** 10 g; **Protein:** 6 g; **Saturated Fat:** 1.5 g; **Cholesterol:** 0 mg; **Sugars:** 4 g.

NOTES: You can add other vegetables like zucchini, carrots, or avocado for varied flavor and texture.
Store the salad in an airtight container in the refrigerator for up to 3 days.

14. Turkey Meatballs with Tomato Sauce

Description

These turkey meatballs with tomato sauce are perfect for health-conscious individuals looking for a protein-rich, low-fat meal. Easy to prepare and delicious, they're ideal for a nutritious lunch or dinner.

Ingredients

For the Turkey Meatballs:
- 1 lb (450 g) ground turkey
- ½ cup (50 g) whole wheat breadcrumbs
- ¼ cup (25 g) grated Parmesan cheese
- 1 large egg
- 2 garlic cloves, minced
- 1 tablespoon (15 g) fresh parsley, chopped
- 1 teaspoon (5 g) dried oregano
- Salt and pepper to taste

For the Tomato Sauce:
- 1 tablespoon (15 ml) extra virgin olive oil
- 1 small onion, chopped
- 3 garlic cloves, minced
- 1 can (28 oz / 800 g) whole peeled tomatoes
- 1 teaspoon (5 g) sugar
- 1 teaspoon (5 g) dried oregano
- ½ teaspoon (2.5 g) red pepper flakes (optional)
- Salt and pepper to taste
- Fresh basil leaves for garnish (optional)

Instructions

Prep Time: 15 min. | **Cooking Time:** 30 min. | **Total Time:** 45 min. | **Difficulty:** Easy

For the Turkey Meatballs:
1. Preheat the oven to 400°F (200°C) and line a baking sheet with parchment paper.
2. In a large bowl, mix together the ground turkey, breadcrumbs, Parmesan, egg, garlic, parsley, oregano, salt, and pepper.
3. Form the mixture into meatballs (about 1 1/2 inches in diameter) and place them on the prepared baking sheet.
4. Bake the meatballs in the oven for 20-25 minutes, or until they are golden brown and fully cooked.

For the Tomato Sauce:
1. While the meatballs are baking, heat the olive oil in a large skillet over medium heat.
2. Add the onion and cook for 5-7 min., until softened and translucent.
3. Add the garlic and cook for 1 minute, until fragrant.
4. Add the whole peeled tomatoes, sugar, oregano, red pepper flakes (if using), salt, and pepper.
5. Bring to a boil, then reduce the heat and simmer for 15-20 min., stirring occasionally.

Assembly:
1. Add the cooked meatballs to the tomato sauce and cook for another 5 min., allowing the flavors to meld.
2. Serve hot, garnished with fresh basil leaves, if desired.

Nutritional Information per Serving (about 4 meatballs with sauce)

Calories: 300; **Carbohydrates:** 18 g; **Fat:** 15 g; **Protein:** 25 g; **Saturated Fat:** 4 g; **Cholesterol:** 100 mg; **Sugars:** 8 g.

NOTES: You can serve the turkey meatballs with whole wheat spaghetti or over a bed of vegetables for a complete and balanced meal.

Store leftovers in an airtight container in the refrigerator for up to 3 days or freeze for up to 3 months.

15. Barley Salad with Grilled Vegetables

Description

This barley salad with grilled vegetables is perfect for health-conscious individuals looking for a light, fiber-rich, and low-fat meal. Easy to prepare and delicious, it's ideal for a nutritious lunch or dinner.

Ingredients

- 1 cup (200 g) pearl barley
- 3 cups (720 ml) water or low-sodium vegetable broth
- 1 medium zucchini, sliced
- 1 red bell pepper, sliced
- 1 small eggplant, sliced
- 1 red onion, sliced
- 1 cup (150 g) cherry tomatoes, halved
- 2 tablespoons (30 ml) extra virgin olive oil
- 1 tablespoon (15 ml) balsamic vinegar
- 1 teaspoon (5 ml) Dijon mustard
- 2 garlic cloves, minced
- Salt and pepper to taste
- ¼ cup (15 g) fresh parsley, chopped
- Fresh basil leaves for garnish (optional)

Instructions

Prep Time: 15 min. | **Cooking Time:** 30 min. | **Total Time:** 45 min. | **Difficulty:** Easy

1. Rinse the barley under cold running water. In a medium saucepan, bring the water or vegetable broth to a boil. Add the barley, reduce the heat, cover, and simmer for about 25-30 minutes, or until the barley is tender. Drain and let cool.
2. Preheat a grill or grill pan to medium-high heat.
3. Brush the zucchini, bell pepper, eggplant, and onion slices with some olive oil and season with salt and pepper.
4. Grill the vegetables for 3-4 minutes per side, or until tender and slightly charred. Let cool slightly and cut into smaller pieces.
5. In a large bowl, combine the cooked barley, grilled vegetables, and cherry tomatoes.
6. In a small bowl, whisk together the remaining olive oil, balsamic vinegar, Dijon mustard, garlic, salt, and pepper.
7. Pour the dressing over the salad and toss well to combine.
8. Garnish with chopped fresh parsley and basil leaves, if desired.
9. Serve immediately or refrigerate until ready to serve.

Nutritional Information per Serving (about 1 cup / 240 g)

Calories: 220; **Carbohydrates:** 35 g; **Fat:** 8 g; **Protein:** 5 g; **Saturated Fat:** 1 g; **Cholesterol:** 0 mg; **Sugars:** 5 g.

NOTES: You can add other vegetables like carrots, green beans, or mushrooms for varied flavor and texture. Store the salad in an airtight container in the refrigerator for up to 3 days.

Dinner Recipes

1. Baked Salmon with Asparagus

Description
This baked salmon with asparagus dish is perfect for health-conscious individuals looking for a protein-rich meal with healthy fats but low in saturated fats. Easy to prepare and delicious, it's ideal for a nutritious lunch or dinner.

Ingredients
- 4 salmon fillets (about 4 oz / 115 g each)
- 1 bunch of asparagus, trimmed
- 2 tablespoons (30 ml) extra virgin olive oil
- 2 garlic cloves, minced
- Juice of 1 lemon
- Zest of 1 lemon
- 1 teaspoon (5 g) fresh thyme, chopped (or ½ teaspoon dried thyme)
- Salt and pepper to taste
- Lemon slices for garnish (optional)

Instructions

Prep Time: 10 min. **Cooking Time:** 20 min. **Total Time:** 30 min. **Difficulty:** Easy

1. Preheat the oven to 400°F (200°C).
2. Arrange the salmon fillets on a baking sheet lined with parchment paper.
3. Arrange the asparagus spears next to the salmon fillets on the baking sheet.
4. In a small bowl, mix together the olive oil, minced garlic, lemon juice, lemon zest, and thyme.
5. Brush the olive oil mixture over the salmon fillets and asparagus. Season with salt and pepper to taste.
6. Bake in the oven for 15-20 minutes, or until the salmon is cooked through and flakes easily with a fork, and the asparagus is tender.
7. Serve warm, garnished with lemon slices if desired.

Nutritional Information per Serving (1 salmon fillet and a portion of asparagus)
Calories: 350; **Carbohydrates:** 5 g; **Fat:** 25 g; **Protein:** 28 g; **Saturated Fat:** 4 g; **Cholesterol:** 70 mg; **Sugars:** 2 g.

NOTES: You can add other vegetables like cherry tomatoes or sweet potatoes for varied flavor and texture. Store leftovers in an airtight container in the refrigerator for up to 3 days.

2. Lemon and Herb Chicken

Description
This lemon and herb chicken dish is perfect for health-conscious individuals looking for a protein-rich, low-fat meal. Easy to prepare and delicious, it's ideal for a nutritious lunch or dinner.

Ingredients
- 4 boneless, skinless chicken breasts (about 4 oz / 115 g each)
- 2 tablespoons (30 ml) extra virgin olive oil
- Juice of 2 lemons
- Zest of 1 lemon
- 2 garlic cloves, minced
- 1 teaspoon (5 g) fresh thyme, chopped (or ½ teaspoon dried thyme)
- 1 teaspoon (5 g) fresh rosemary, chopped (or ½ teaspoon dried rosemary)
- Salt and pepper to taste
- Lemon slices for garnish (optional)
- Fresh parsley, chopped, for garnish (optional)

Instructions

Prep Time: 10 min.	Marinating Time: 30 min.	Cooking Time: 20 min.	Total Time: 1 hour	Difficulty: Easy

1. In a large bowl, mix together the olive oil, lemon juice, lemon zest, garlic, thyme, rosemary, salt, and pepper.
2. Add the chicken breasts to the bowl and toss well to ensure they are fully coated in the marinade. Cover and refrigerate for at least 30 minutes.
3. Preheat the oven to 375°F (190°C).
4. Transfer the chicken breasts to a baking sheet lined with parchment paper.
5. Bake in the oven for 20-25 minutes, or until the chicken is cooked through and the juices run clear.
6. Garnish with lemon slices and fresh parsley, if desired.
7. Serve warm.

Nutritional Information per Serving (1 chicken breast)
Calories: 220; **Carbohydrates:** 2 g; **Fat:** 10 g; **Protein:** 28 g; **Saturated Fat:** 1.5 g; **Cholesterol:** 75 mg; **Sugars:** 0 g.

NOTES: You can add other fresh herbs like basil or oregano for varied flavor.
Store leftovers in an airtight container in the refrigerator for up to 3 days.

3. Vegetable and Bean Soup

Description

This vegetable and bean soup is perfect for health-conscious individuals looking for a nutrient-rich, low-fat meal. Easy to prepare and delicious, it's ideal for a light and nutritious lunch or dinner.

Ingredients

- 2 tablespoons (30 ml) extra virgin olive oil
- 1 medium onion, chopped
- 2 carrots, peeled and diced
- 2 celery stalks, diced
- 3 garlic cloves, minced
- 1 medium zucchini, diced
- 1 red bell pepper, diced
- 1 cup (150 g) green beans, cut into pieces
- 1 can (14 oz / 400 g) diced tomatoes
- 6 cups (1.4 L) low-sodium vegetable broth
- 1 can (15 oz / 425 g) cannellini beans, drained and rinsed
- 1 can (15 oz / 425 g) black beans, drained and rinsed
- 1 teaspoon (5 g) dried thyme
- 1 teaspoon (5 g) dried oregano
- 1 bay leaf
- Salt and pepper to taste
- ½ cup (50 g) whole wheat pasta (optional)
- Grated Parmesan cheese for serving (optional)
- Fresh basil leaves for garnish (optional)

Instructions

Prep Time: 15 min.   **Cooking Time:** 30 min.   **Total Time:** 45 min.   **Difficulty:** Easy

1. In a large pot, heat the olive oil over medium heat.
2. Add the onion, carrots, and celery. Cook for 5-7 minutes, until the vegetables are tender.
3. Add the garlic and cook for 1 minute, until fragrant.
4. Add the zucchini, red bell pepper, and green beans. Cook for another 5 minutes.
5. Add the diced tomatoes, vegetable broth, cannellini beans, black beans, thyme, oregano, and bay leaf. Bring to a boil.
6. Reduce the heat and simmer for 15-20 minutes, until the vegetables are tender.
7. If using pasta, add it during the last 10 minutes of cooking.
8. Remove the bay leaf and season with salt and pepper to taste.
9. Serve hot, with grated Parmesan cheese and fresh basil leaves, if desired.

Nutritional Information per Serving (about 1 cup / 240 g)

Calories: 250; **Carbohydrates:** 40 g; **Fat:** 7 g; **Protein:** 10 g; **Saturated Fat:** 1 g; **Cholesterol:** 0 mg; **Sugars:** 6 g.

NOTES: You can add other vegetables like spinach, broccoli, or kale for varied flavor and increased nutritional content.
Store leftover soup in an airtight container in the refrigerator for up to 5 days, or freeze for up to 3 months.

4. Tofu Stir-Fry with Vegetables

Description

This tofu and vegetable stir-fry is perfect for health-conscious individuals looking for a light, plant-based protein meal that's low in fat. Easy to prepare and delicious, it's ideal for a nutritious lunch or dinner.

Ingredients

- 1 block (14 oz / 400 g) extra-firm tofu, drained and cubed
- 2 tablespoons (30 ml) sesame oil or olive oil
- 1 medium onion, thinly sliced
- 2 carrots, peeled and julienned
- 1 red bell pepper, sliced into strips
- 1 medium zucchini, sliced into rounds
- 1 cup (150 g) broccoli florets
- 2 garlic cloves, minced
- 1 tablespoon (15 g) grated fresh ginger
- ¼ cup (60 ml) low-sodium soy sauce
- 2 tablespoons (30 ml) oyster sauce (optional)
- 1 tablespoon (15 ml) rice vinegar
- 1 teaspoon (5 ml) toasted sesame oil (optional)
- 1 tablespoon (15 g) sesame seeds for garnish (optional)
- Sliced green onions for garnish (optional)

Instructions

Prep Time: 15 min. **Cooking Time:** 15 min. **Total Time:** 30 min. **Difficulty:** Easy

1. Heat 1 tablespoon of sesame oil in a large skillet or wok over medium-high heat.
2. Add the cubed tofu and cook for 5-7 minutes, turning occasionally, until golden brown on all sides. Remove the tofu from the skillet and set aside.
3. In the same skillet, add the remaining tablespoon of sesame oil. Add the onion, carrots, red bell pepper, zucchini, and broccoli. Cook for 5-7 minutes, stirring frequently, until the vegetables are tender-crisp.
4. Add the minced garlic and grated ginger and cook for 1 minute, until fragrant.
5. Return the tofu to the skillet. Add the soy sauce, oyster sauce (if using), rice vinegar, and toasted sesame oil (if using). Stir well to combine all ingredients.
6. Cook for an additional 2-3 minutes, stirring frequently, until everything is well combined and heated through.
7. Garnish with sesame seeds and sliced green onions, if desired.
8. Serve hot with brown rice or noodles.

Nutritional Information per Serving (about 1 cup / 240 g)

Calories: 250; **Carbohydrates:** 18 g; **Fat:** 14 g; **Protein:** 15 g; **Saturated Fat:** 2 g; **Cholesterol:** 0 mg; **Sugars:** 6 g.

NOTES: You can add other vegetables like mushrooms, spinach, or green beans for varied flavor and texture. Store leftovers in an airtight container in the refrigerator for up to 3 days.

5. Spinach and Smoked Salmon Salad

Description

This spinach and smoked salmon salad is perfect for health-conscious individuals looking for a light, protein-rich meal with healthy fats but low in saturated fats. Easy to prepare and delicious, it's ideal for a nutritious lunch or dinner.

Ingredients

- 4 cups (120 g) fresh spinach
- 8 oz (225 g) smoked salmon, sliced
- 1 avocado, sliced
- 1 medium cucumber, sliced into rounds
- ½ red onion, thinly sliced
- ¼ cup (30 g) capers, drained
- ¼ cup (60 ml) extra virgin olive oil
- 2 tablespoons (30 ml) fresh lemon juice
- 1 teaspoon (5 g) Dijon mustard
- Salt and pepper to taste
- Lemon slices for garnish (optional)

Instructions

Prep Time: 10 min.   **Cooking Time:** 0 min.   **Total Time:** 10 min.   **Difficulty:** Easy

1. In a large bowl, combine the spinach, smoked salmon, avocado, cucumber, red onion, and capers.
2. In a small bowl, whisk together the olive oil, lemon juice, Dijon mustard, salt, and pepper.
3. Pour the dressing over the salad and gently toss to combine.
4. Garnish with lemon slices, if desired.
5. Serve immediately.

Nutritional Information per Serving (about 1 cup / 240 g)

Calories: 300; **Carbohydrates:** 10 g; **Fat:** 24 g; **Protein:** 12 g; **Saturated Fat:** 3 g; **Cholesterol:** 25 mg; **Sugars:** 2 g.

NOTES: You can add other vegetables like cherry tomatoes, radishes, or bell peppers for varied flavor and texture. Store the salad in an airtight container in the refrigerator for up to 1 day, but it's best consumed immediately to maintain freshness

6. Chicken Fajitas

Description
These chicken fajitas are perfect for health-conscious individuals looking for a protein-rich, low-fat meal. Easy to prepare and full of flavor, they're ideal for a nutritious lunch or dinner.

Ingredients
- 1 lb (450 g) boneless, skinless chicken breasts, cut into strips
- 2 tablespoons (30 ml) olive oil
- 1 teaspoon (5 g) paprika
- 1 teaspoon (5 g) ground cumin
- ½ teaspoon (2.5 g) garlic powder
- ½ teaspoon (2.5 g) onion powder
- ½ teaspoon (2.5 g) chili powder
- Juice of 1 lime
- Salt and pepper to taste
- 1 red bell pepper, sliced into strips
- 1 green bell pepper, sliced into strips
- 1 medium onion, thinly sliced
- 8 whole wheat tortillas
- ½ cup (120 g) low-sodium salsa
- ½ cup (120 g) low-fat Greek yogurt
- Fresh cilantro leaves for garnish (optional)
- Lime wedges for serving

Instructions

| **Prep Time:** 15 min. | **Cooking Time:** 15 min. | **Total Time:** 30 min. | **Difficulty:** Easy |

1. In a large bowl, mix together the olive oil, paprika, cumin, garlic powder, onion powder, chili powder, lime juice, salt, and pepper.
2. Add the chicken strips to the bowl and mix well to ensure they are fully coated in the marinade. Let sit for 10 minutes.
3. Heat a large skillet over medium-high heat. Add the marinated chicken and cook for 5-7 minutes, or until the chicken is fully cooked.
4. Remove the chicken from the skillet and set aside. In the same skillet, add the bell peppers and onion. Cook for 5-7 minutes, until the vegetables are tender-crisp.
5. Return the chicken to the skillet with the vegetables and mix well to combine.
6. Warm the tortillas in a dry skillet or in the microwave.
7. Assemble the fajitas by placing the chicken and vegetables in the center of each tortilla. Add a spoonful of salsa and Greek yogurt.
8. Garnish with fresh cilantro leaves and serve with lime wedges.

Nutritional Information per Serving (1 fajita)
Calories: 250; **Carbohydrates:** 30 g; **Fat:** 8 g; **Protein:** 20 g; **Saturated Fat:** 2 g; **Cholesterol:** 45 mg; **Sugars:** 4 g.

NOTES: You can add other vegetables like zucchini or mushrooms for varied flavor and texture.
Store leftovers in an airtight container in the refrigerator for up to 3 days.

7. Almond-Crusted Cod

Description
This almond-crusted cod is perfect for health-conscious individuals looking for a protein-rich meal with healthy fats but low in saturated fats. Easy to prepare and delicious, it's ideal for a nutritious lunch or dinner.

Ingredients
- 4 cod fillets (about 4 oz / 115 g each)
- ½ cup (60 g) finely chopped almonds
- ¼ cup (30 g) whole wheat breadcrumbs
- ¼ cup (25 g) grated Parmesan cheese
- 1 teaspoon (5 g) paprika
- 1 teaspoon (5 g) garlic powder
- 1 teaspoon (5 g) onion powder
- 1 teaspoon (5 g) dried thyme
- Salt and pepper to taste
- 2 tablespoons (30 ml) extra virgin olive oil
- Juice of 1 lemon
- Lemon slices for garnish (optional)
- Fresh parsley, chopped, for garnish (optional)

Instructions

Prep Time: 15 min.   **Cooking Time:** 20 min.   **Total Time:** 35 min.   **Difficulty:** Easy

1. Preheat the oven to 400°F (200°C) and line a baking sheet with parchment paper.
2. In a medium bowl, mix together the chopped almonds, breadcrumbs, Parmesan cheese, paprika, garlic powder, onion powder, thyme, salt, and pepper.
3. Brush the cod fillets with olive oil and squeeze lemon juice over them.
4. Dredge each fillet in the almond mixture, pressing gently to adhere the crust.
5. Place the fillets on the prepared baking sheet and bake for 15-20 minutes, or until the fish is cooked through and the crust is golden brown.
6. Serve warm, garnished with lemon slices and fresh parsley, if desired.

Nutritional Information per Serving (1 fillet)
Calories: 320; **Carbohydrates:** 8 g; **Fat:** 20 g; **Protein:** 28 g; **Saturated Fat:** 3 g; **Cholesterol:** 60 mg; **Sugars:** 2 g.

NOTES: You can serve the cod with sides of grilled vegetables or a fresh salad for a complete and balanced meal. Store leftovers in an airtight container in the refrigerator for up to 2 days.

8. Zucchini Spaghetti with Pesto

Description

This zucchini spaghetti with pesto is perfect for health-conscious individuals looking for a light, nutrient-rich, and low-fat meal. Easy to prepare and delicious, it's ideal for a nutritious lunch or dinner.

Ingredients

- 4 medium zucchinis, spiralized or julienned into zucchini noodles
- 1 cup (240 ml) homemade or store-bought pesto
- ¼ cup (30 g) toasted pine nuts
- ¼ cup (25 g) grated Parmesan cheese
- 1 tablespoon (15 ml) extra virgin olive oil
- 2 garlic cloves, minced
- Juice of 1 lemon
- Salt and pepper to taste
- Fresh basil leaves for garnish (optional)
- Ingredients for the Pesto (if homemade)
- 2 cups (60 g) fresh basil leaves
- ½ cup (120 ml) extra virgin olive oil
- ¼ cup (30 g) pine nuts
- ¼ cup (25 g) grated Parmesan cheese
- 2 garlic cloves
- Salt and pepper to taste

Instructions for the Pesto (if homemade)

1. In a food processor, combine the basil, pine nuts, Parmesan, and garlic. Blend until smooth.
2. With the processor running, slowly add the olive oil until the mixture is creamy.
3. Season with salt and pepper to taste. Set aside.

Instructions

| **Prep Time:** 15 min. | **Cooking Time:** 5 min. | **Total Time:** 20 min. | **Difficulty:** Easy |

1. In a large skillet, heat the olive oil over medium heat. Add the minced garlic and cook for 1 minute, until fragrant.
2. Add the zucchini noodles to the skillet and cook for 2-3 minutes, stirring gently, until slightly softened but still crisp.
3. Remove the skillet from the heat and add the pesto, lemon juice, salt, and pepper. Toss well to combine.
4. Transfer the zucchini noodles to serving plates. Garnish with toasted pine nuts, grated Parmesan cheese, and fresh basil leaves, if desired.
5. Serve immediately.

Nutritional Information per Serving (about 1 cup / 240 g)

Calories: 250; **Carbohydrates:** 8 g; **Fat:** 22 g; **Protein:** 6 g; **Saturated Fat:** 3 g; **Cholesterol:** 10 mg; **Sugars:** 5 g.

NOTES: You can add other vegetables like cherry tomatoes, bell peppers, or mushrooms for varied flavor and texture. Store leftovers in an airtight container in the refrigerator for up to 2 days.

9. Turkey and Bean Chili

Description

This turkey and bean chili is perfect for health-conscious individuals looking for a protein-rich, fiber-packed, and low-fat meal. Easy to prepare and delicious, it's ideal for a nutritious lunch or dinner.

Ingredients

- 1 lb (450 g) lean ground turkey
- 1 tablespoon (15 ml) olive oil
- 1 medium onion, chopped
- 3 garlic cloves, minced
- 1 red bell pepper, diced
- 1 green bell pepper, diced
- 1 can (15 oz / 425 g) black beans, drained and rinsed
- 1 can (15 oz / 425 g) kidney beans, drained and rinsed
- 1 can (15 oz / 425 g) diced tomatoes
- 1 can (6 oz / 170 g) tomato paste
- 2 cups (480 ml) low-sodium chicken broth
- 2 tablespoons (30 g) chili powder
- 1 tablespoon (15 g) ground cumin
- 1 teaspoon (5 g) smoked paprika
- 1 teaspoon (5 g) dried oregano
- ½ teaspoon (2.5 g) cayenne pepper (optional)
- Salt and pepper to taste
- Juice of 1 lime
- Fresh cilantro, chopped, for garnish (optional)

Instructions

Prep Time: 15 min. **Cooking Time:** 45 min. **Total Time:** 1 hour **Difficulty:** Easy

1. In a large pot, heat the olive oil over medium-high heat. Add the ground turkey and cook for 5-7 minutes, until fully cooked and browned. Break the turkey into smaller pieces as it cooks.
2. Add the onion, garlic, red bell pepper, and green bell pepper to the pot. Cook for another 5-7 minutes, until the vegetables are tender.
3. Add the black beans, kidney beans, diced tomatoes, tomato paste, chicken broth, chili powder, cumin, smoked paprika, oregano, cayenne pepper (if using), salt, and pepper.
4. Bring to a boil, then reduce the heat and simmer for 30 minutes, stirring occasionally.
5. Add the lime juice and stir well.
6. Serve hot, garnished with fresh cilantro, if desired.

Nutritional Information per Serving (about 1 cup / 240 g)

Calories: 300; **Carbohydrates:** 30 g; **Fat:** 8 g; **Protein:** 28 g; **Saturated Fat:** 1.5 g; **Cholesterol:** 55 mg; **Sugars:** 6 g.

NOTES: You can add other vegetables like zucchini, corn, or carrots for varied flavor and texture. Store the chili in an airtight container in the refrigerator for up to 5 days, or freeze for up to 3 months.

10. Risotto with Mushrooms

Description
This mushroom risotto is perfect for health-conscious individuals looking for a flavorful, creamy, and low-fat meal. Easy to prepare and delicious, it's ideal for a nutritious lunch or dinner.

Ingredients
- 1½ cups (300 g) Arborio rice
- 4 cups (1 liter) low-sodium vegetable broth
- 1 tablespoon (15 ml) extra virgin olive oil
- 1 small onion, finely chopped
- 3 garlic cloves, minced
- 1 cup (240 ml) dry white wine
- 1 lb (450 g) mixed mushrooms (button, cremini, porcini), sliced
- ¼ cup (25 g) grated Parmesan cheese
- ¼ cup (30 g) fresh parsley, chopped
- Salt and pepper to taste
- Grated lemon zest for garnish (optional)

Instructions

Prep Time: 10 min.   **Cooking Time:** 30 min.   **Total Time:** 40 min.   **Difficulty:** Medium

1. In a medium saucepan, heat the vegetable broth over low heat, keeping it warm but not boiling.
2. In a large skillet, heat the olive oil over medium heat. Add the onion and cook for 5-7 minutes, until translucent.
3. Add the garlic and cook for 1 minute, until fragrant.
4. Add the Arborio rice and stir well to lightly toast it, about 2 minutes.
5. Pour in the white wine and cook, stirring continuously, until the liquid is fully absorbed.
6. Add a ladleful of warm broth to the rice and stir until almost fully absorbed. Continue adding the broth, one ladleful at a time, stirring continuously, until the rice is creamy and al dente, about 20 minutes.
7. Meanwhile, in a separate skillet, cook the sliced mushrooms over medium-high heat until golden and tender, about 5-7 minutes. Season with salt and pepper to taste.
8. When the risotto is nearly done, stir in the cooked mushrooms.
9. Remove the skillet from the heat and stir in the grated Parmesan cheese and chopped parsley. Adjust seasoning with salt and pepper if necessary.
10. Serve warm, garnished with grated lemon zest, if desired.

Nutritional Information per Serving (about 1 cup / 240 g)
Calories: 350; **Carbohydrates:** 50 g; **Fat:** 8 g; **Protein:** 10 g; **Saturated Fat:** 2 g; **Cholesterol:** 10 mg; **Sugars:** 3 g.

NOTES: You can add other vegetables like spinach or peas to increase the nutritional content.
Store leftovers in an airtight container in the refrigerator for up to 3 days.

11. Lentil Meatballs

Description
These lentil meatballs are perfect for health-conscious individuals looking for a meal rich in plant-based protein, fiber, and low in fat. Easy to prepare and delicious, they're ideal for a nutritious lunch or dinner.

Ingredients
- 1 cup (200 g) dried lentils
- 2½ cups (600 ml) water
- 1 small onion, finely chopped
- 2 garlic cloves, minced
- 1 medium carrot, grated
- ½ cup (50 g) whole wheat breadcrumbs
- ¼ cup (30 g) grated Parmesan cheese
- 2 tablespoons (30 g) tomato paste
- 1 teaspoon (5 g) dried oregano
- 1 teaspoon (5 g) ground cumin
- ½ teaspoon (2.5 g) black pepper
- ½ teaspoon (2.5 g) salt
- 1 large egg
- 2 tablespoons (30 ml) olive oil
- For the Tomato Sauce:
- 1 tablespoon (15 ml) olive oil
- 1 small onion, chopped
- 2 garlic cloves, minced
- 1 can (14 oz / 400 g) whole peeled tomatoes
- 1 teaspoon (5 g) sugar
- 1 teaspoon (5 g) dried oregano
- Salt and pepper to taste
- Fresh basil leaves for garnish (optional)

Instructions

Prep Time: 20 min. **Cooking Time:** 40 min. **Total Time:** 1 hour **Difficulty:** Medium

For the Lentil Meatballs:
1. Rinse the lentils under cold running water. In a medium pot, bring the lentils and water to a boil. Reduce the heat, cover, and simmer for 20-25 minutes, or until the lentils are tender. Drain and let cool.
2. In a large bowl, combine the cooked lentils, onion, garlic, carrot, breadcrumbs, Parmesan, tomato paste, oregano, cumin, black pepper, salt, and egg. Mix well until the mixture is uniform.
3. Form the mixture into meatballs (about 1 1/2 inches in diameter).
4. In a large skillet, heat the olive oil over medium heat. Add the meatballs and cook for 7-10 minutes, turning occasionally, until golden brown on all sides.

For the Tomato Sauce:
1. In a medium saucepan, heat the olive oil over medium heat. Add the onion and cook for 5-7 min., until translucent.
2. Add the garlic and cook for 1 minute, until fragrant.
3. Add the whole peeled tomatoes, sugar, oregano, salt, and pepper. Bring to a boil, then reduce the heat and simmer for 20-25 min., stirring occasionally.

Assembly:
1. Add the lentil meatballs to the tomato sauce and cook for another 5-10 min., allowing the flavors to meld.
2. Serve hot, garnished with fresh basil leaves, if desired.

Nutritional Information per Serving (about 3-4 meatballs with sauce)
Calories: 300; **Carbohydrates:** 40 g; **Fat:** 10 g; **Protein:** 14 g; **Saturated Fat:** 2 g; **Cholesterol:** 30 mg; **Sugars:** 8 g.

NOTES: You can serve the lentil meatballs with whole wheat spaghetti or over a bed of vegetables for a complete and balanced meal.
Store leftovers in an airtight container in the refrigerator for up to 3 days or freeze for up to 3 months.

12. Chicken and Avocado Salad

Description

This chicken and avocado salad is perfect for health-conscious individuals looking for a light, protein-rich meal with healthy fats but low in saturated fats. Easy to prepare and delicious, it's ideal for a nutritious lunch or dinner.

Ingredients

- 2 boneless, skinless chicken breasts (about 8 oz / 225 g each)
- 1 tablespoon (15 ml) extra virgin olive oil
- Salt and pepper to taste
- 1 teaspoon (5 g) paprika
- 1 teaspoon (5 g) garlic powder
- 1 teaspoon (5 g) ground cumin
- 6 cups (180 g) mixed greens or fresh spinach
- 1 ripe avocado, sliced
- 1 medium cucumber, sliced into rounds
- ½ red onion, thinly sliced
- ¼ cup (30 g) cherry tomatoes, halved
- Juice of 1 lime
- ¼ cup (60 ml) extra virgin olive oil
- 1 tablespoon (15 ml) apple cider vinegar
- Salt and pepper to taste
- Fresh cilantro leaves for garnish (optional)

Instructions

Prep Time: 15 min. | **Cooking Time:** 15 min. | **Total Time:** 30 min. | **Difficulty:** Easy

1. Preheat a grill or grill pan to medium-high heat.
2. Season the chicken breasts with olive oil, salt, pepper, paprika, garlic powder, and cumin.
3. Grill the chicken breasts for 6-7 minutes per side, or until fully cooked and the juices run clear. Let cool slightly, then slice.
4. In a large bowl, combine the mixed greens, avocado, cucumber, red onion, and cherry tomatoes.
5. In a small bowl, whisk together the lime juice, olive oil, and apple cider vinegar. Season with salt and pepper to taste.
6. Pour the dressing over the salad and gently toss to combine.
7. Top the salad with the sliced grilled chicken.
8. Garnish with fresh cilantro leaves, if desired.
9. Serve immediately.

Nutritional Information per Serving (about 2 cups / 480 g)

Calories: 350; **Carbohydrates:** 10 g; **Fat:** 25 g; **Protein:** 25 g; **Saturated Fat:** 3.5 g; **Cholesterol:** 60 mg; **Sugars:** 2 g.

NOTES: You can add other vegetables like bell peppers, radishes, or carrots for varied flavor and texture.
Store the salad without dressing in an airtight container in the refrigerator for up to 2 days and add the dressing just before serving.

13. Grilled Shrimp with Vegetables

Description
This grilled shrimp with vegetables dish is perfect for health-conscious individuals looking for a light, protein-rich meal that is low in saturated fats. Easy to prepare and delicious, it's ideal for a nutritious lunch or dinner.

Ingredients
- 1 lb (450 g) large shrimp, peeled and deveined
- 2 tablespoons (30 ml) extra virgin olive oil
- Juice of 1 lemon
- 3 garlic cloves, minced
- 1 teaspoon (5 g) paprika
- 1 teaspoon (5 g) dried oregano
- 1 red bell pepper, sliced into strips
- 1 yellow bell pepper, sliced into strips
- 1 medium zucchini, sliced into rounds
- 1 red onion, cut into wedges
- 1 cup (150 g) cherry tomatoes, halved
- Salt and pepper to taste
- Fresh parsley leaves for garnish (optional)

Instructions

Prep Time: 15 min.   **Cooking Time:** 15 min.   **Total Time:** 30 min.   **Difficulty:** Easy

1. In a large bowl, mix together the olive oil, lemon juice, minced garlic, paprika, oregano, salt, and pepper. Add the shrimp and toss to coat. Let marinate for 10 minutes.
2. Preheat a grill or grill pan to medium-high heat.
3. Grill the shrimp for 2-3 minutes per side, or until they are opaque and cooked through.
4. Meanwhile, in a large bowl, toss the bell pepper strips, zucchini rounds, red onion wedges, and cherry tomatoes with a bit of olive oil, salt, and pepper.
5. Grill the vegetables for 5-7 minutes, turning occasionally, until they are tender and slightly charred.
6. Serve the grilled shrimp over the grilled vegetables.
7. Garnish with fresh parsley leaves, if desired.
8. Serve immediately.

Nutritional Information per Serving (about 1 cup / 240 g)
Calories: 250; **Carbohydrates:** 12 g; **Fat:** 10 g; **Protein:** 28 g; **Saturated Fat:** 1.5 g; **Cholesterol:** 190 mg; **Sugars:** 6 g.

NOTES: You can add other vegetables like mushrooms, asparagus, or carrots for varied flavor and texture.
Store leftovers in an airtight container in the refrigerator for up to 2 days.

14. Kale and Quinoa Salad

Description
This kale and quinoa salad is perfect for health-conscious individuals looking for a nutrient-rich meal with plenty of protein and fiber, but low in saturated fats. Easy to prepare and delicious, it's ideal for a nutritious lunch or dinner.

Ingredients
- 1 cup (170 g) quinoa
- 2 cups (480 ml) water
- 4 cups (120 g) kale, chopped
- 1 cup (150 g) cherry tomatoes, halved
- 1 medium cucumber, sliced
- ¼ cup (30 g) sliced almonds, toasted
- ¼ cup (30 g) raisins
- 1 avocado, sliced
- ¼ cup (60 ml) extra virgin olive oil
- 2 tablespoons (30 ml) fresh lemon juice
- 1 tablespoon (15 ml) apple cider vinegar
- 1 teaspoon (5 g) Dijon mustard
- 1 garlic clove, minced
- Salt and pepper to taste

Instructions

Prep Time: 15 min.   **Cooking Time:** 15 min.   **Total Time:** 30 min.   **Difficulty:** Easy

1. Rinse the quinoa under cold running water. In a medium saucepan, bring the water to a boil, add the quinoa, reduce the heat, cover, and simmer for about 15 minutes, or until the water is absorbed and the quinoa is tender. Let cool.
2. In a large bowl, combine the chopped kale, cherry tomatoes, cucumber, toasted almonds, raisins, and sliced avocado.
3. In a small bowl, whisk together the olive oil, lemon juice, apple cider vinegar, Dijon mustard, minced garlic, salt, and pepper.
4. Add the cooled quinoa to the bowl with the vegetables.
5. Pour the dressing over the salad and gently toss to combine.
6. Serve immediately or refrigerate until ready to serve.

Nutritional Information per Serving (about 1 cup / 240 g)
Calories: 350; **Carbohydrates:** 38 g; **Fat:** 20 g; **Protein:** 9 g; **Saturated Fat:** 2.5 g; **Cholesterol:** 0 mg; **Sugars:** 6 g.

NOTES: You can add other vegetables like bell peppers, carrots, or radishes for varied flavor and texture.
Store the salad in an airtight container in the refrigerator for up to 2 days.

15. Baked Tofu with Vegetables

Description

This baked tofu with vegetables dish is perfect for health-conscious individuals looking for a light, plant-based protein meal that is low in saturated fats. Easy to prepare and delicious, it's ideal for a nutritious lunch or dinner.

Ingredients

- 1 block (14 oz / 400 g) extra-firm tofu, drained and pressed
- 2 tablespoons (30 ml) extra virgin olive oil
- 2 tablespoons (30 ml) low-sodium soy sauce
- 1 tablespoon (15 ml) maple syrup
- 1 tablespoon (15 ml) rice vinegar
- 1 teaspoon (5 g) garlic powder
- 1 teaspoon (5 g) ground ginger
- 1 red bell pepper, sliced into strips
- 1 medium zucchini, sliced into rounds
- 1 large carrot, julienned
- 1 red onion, cut into wedges
- 1 cup (150 g) broccoli florets
- Sesame seeds for garnish (optional)
- Sliced green onions for garnish (optional)

Instructions

Prep Time: 15 min. **Cooking Time:** 30 min. **Total Time:** 45 min. **Difficulty:** Easy

1. Preheat the oven to 400°F (200°C) and line a baking sheet with parchment paper.
2. Cut the pressed tofu into 1-inch cubes. In a medium bowl, mix together the olive oil, soy sauce, maple syrup, rice vinegar, garlic powder, and ground ginger.
3. Add the tofu cubes to the bowl and gently toss to coat evenly. Let marinate for 10 minutes.
4. Spread the marinated tofu cubes on the prepared baking sheet in a single layer. Bake in the oven for 20 minutes, turning the cubes halfway through, until golden and crispy.
5. Meanwhile, in a large bowl, toss the red bell pepper, zucchini, carrot, red onion, and broccoli with a bit of olive oil, salt, and pepper.
6. Spread the vegetables on another parchment-lined baking sheet and bake in the oven for 15-20 minutes, or until the vegetables are tender and slightly browned.
7. Once cooked, combine the tofu and vegetables in a large bowl and gently toss.
8. Garnish with sesame seeds and sliced green onions, if desired.
9. Serve warm.

Nutritional Information per Serving (about 1 cup / 240 g)

Calories: 250; **Carbohydrates:** 18 g; **Fat:** 14 g; **Protein:** 12 g; **Saturated Fat:** 2 g; **Cholesterol:** 0 mg; **Sugars:** 8 g.

NOTES: You can add other vegetables like mushrooms, asparagus, or spinach for varied flavor and texture.
Store leftovers in an airtight container in the refrigerator for up to 3 days.

Snacks & Snacks

1. Low-Fat Chickpea Hummus

Description

This low-fat chickpea hummus is perfect for those looking for a healthy and tasty snack or appetizer. It's creamy, flavorful, and easy to make. Great for pairing with fresh vegetables or whole grain bread.

Ingredients

- 1 can of chickpeas (15 oz / 425 g), drained and rinsed
- ¼ cup (60 ml) fresh lemon juice
- 2 tablespoons (30 ml) water
- 1 tablespoon (15 ml) extra virgin olive oil
- 1 tablespoon (15 g) tahini (optional to further reduce fat content)
- 1 garlic clove, minced
- ½ teaspoon (2.5 g) salt
- ½ teaspoon (2.5 g) ground cumin
- ¼ teaspoon (1.25 g) sweet paprika (for garnish)
- Fresh parsley, chopped (for garnish)

Instructions

Prep Time: 10 min. | **Cooking Time:** 0 min. | **Total Time:** 10 min. | **Difficulty:** Easy

1. In a food processor, combine the chickpeas, lemon juice, water, olive oil, tahini (if using), garlic, salt, and cumin.
2. Blend until smooth and creamy. If needed, add a bit more water to achieve the desired consistency.
3. Transfer the hummus to a bowl and garnish with sweet paprika and chopped fresh parsley.
4. Serve with fresh vegetables or whole grain bread.

Nutritional Information per Serving (about 2 tablespoons / 30 g)

Calories: 50; **Carbohydrates:** 6 g; **Fat:** 2 g; **Protein:** 2 g; **Saturated Fat:** 0.3 g; **Cholesterol:** 0 mg; **Sugars:** 1 g.

NOTES: For an even lighter hummus, omit the tahini and add more lemon juice and water to maintain creaminess. Store the hummus in an airtight container in the refrigerator for up to a week.

2. Green Smoothie

Description

This green smoothie is perfect for health-conscious individuals looking for a nutrient-packed, low-fat breakfast or snack option. Rich in vitamins, minerals, and fiber, it's a delicious way to start your day or recharge in the afternoon.

Ingredients

- 1 cup (240 ml) unsweetened almond milk
- 1 medium banana, frozen
- ½ cup (120 ml) pineapple chunks (fresh or frozen)
- 1 cup (30 g) fresh spinach
- ½ cup (125 g) low-fat Greek yogurt
- 1 teaspoon (5 ml) honey or maple syrup (optional)
- 1 teaspoon (5 g) chia seeds or flaxseeds (optional)

Instructions

Prep Time: 5 min.   **Cooking Time:** 0 min.   **Total Time:** 5 min.   **Difficulty:** Easy

1. Place all ingredients in a blender.
2. Blend until smooth and creamy.
3. Pour into a glass and serve immediately.

Nutritional Information per Serving (about 1 cup / 240 ml)

Calories: 150; **Carbohydrates:** 27 g; **Fat:** 2.5 g; **Protein:** 8 g; **Saturated Fat:** 0.5 g; **Cholesterol:** 5 mg; **Sugars:** 15 g.

NOTES: For an even more nutritious smoothie, add a teaspoon of chia seeds or flaxseeds.
You can substitute almond milk with any other plant-based milk or skim milk.

If you prefer a sweeter taste, add honey or maple syrup.

3. Dried Fruit Bars

Description
These dried fruit bars are perfect for health-conscious individuals looking for an energy-boosting and nutritious snack. They are easy to make, high in fiber, and great for a healthy break during the day.

Ingredients
- 1 cup (140 g) pitted dates
- ½ cup (75 g) dried apricots
- ½ cup (75 g) dried figs
- ½ cup (50 g) chopped nuts
- ¼ cup (30 g) sunflower seeds
- ¼ cup (20 g) unsweetened shredded coconut
- 1 tablespoon (15 ml) honey or maple syrup
- 1 teaspoon (5 ml) vanilla extract

Instructions

Prep Time: 15 min. | **Cooking Time:** 0 min. | **Total Time:** 15 min. | **Difficulty:** Easy

1. In a food processor, chop the dates, apricots, and figs until you get a sticky mixture.
2. Add the nuts, sunflower seeds, and shredded coconut. Blend until all ingredients are well combined.
3. Add the honey (or maple syrup) and vanilla extract. Blend again until the mixture is homogeneous.
4. Transfer the mixture to a baking tray lined with parchment paper. Press the mixture evenly to form a compact layer.
5. Refrigerate for at least an hour to set.
6. Cut into bars of desired size and store in an airtight container in the refrigerator.

Nutritional Information per Bar (about 1 oz / 28 g)
Calories: 120; **Carbohydrates:** 20 g; **Fat:** 4 g; **Protein:** 2 g; **Saturated Fat:** 1 g; **Cholesterol:** 0 mg; **Sugars:** 15 g.

NOTES: You can customize the bars by adding other types of dried fruits or seeds to your liking.
If the mixture is too dry, add a bit of water until you reach the desired consistency.

4. Greek Yogurt with Honey and Nuts

Description

This Greek yogurt with honey and nuts is perfect for health-conscious individuals looking for a high-protein, low-fat breakfast or snack. It's simple, delicious, and nutritious, ideal for starting the day or as an afternoon pick-me-up.

Ingredients

- 1 cup (245 g) low-fat Greek yogurt
- 1 tablespoon (15 ml) honey
- 2 tablespoons (20 g) mixed nuts, chopped (almonds, walnuts, hazelnuts)
- 1 tablespoon (10 g) chia seeds (optional)
- ½ teaspoon (2.5 ml) vanilla extract (optional)
- Fresh fruit (like blueberries, strawberries, or bananas) for garnish (optional)

Instructions

Prep Time: 5 min.   **Cooking Time:** 0 min.   **Total Time:** 5 min.   **Difficulty:** Easy

1. Place the Greek yogurt in a bowl.
2. Add the honey and mix well.
3. Top with the chopped nuts and chia seeds (if using).
4. Add the vanilla extract and fresh fruit if desired.
5. Serve immediately.

Nutritional Information per Serving (about 1 cup / 245 g)

Calories: 220; **Carbohydrates:** 24 g; **Fat:** 8 g; **Protein:** 15 g; **Saturated Fat:** 2 g; **Cholesterol:** 10 mg; **Sugars:** 18 g.

NOTES: You can vary the nuts according to your preference or add other seeds for extra crunch.

If you prefer a less sweet taste, reduce the amount of honey.

Greek yogurt can be substituted with plant-based yogurt for a vegan version.

5. Kale Chips

Description

These kale chips are perfect for health-conscious individuals looking for a crunchy, low-fat snack. They are simple to make, nutrient-rich, and a fantastic alternative to traditional potato chips.

Ingredients

- 1 bunch (about 200 g) of kale
- 1 tablespoon (15 ml) extra virgin olive oil
- ½ teaspoon (2.5 g) sea salt
- ¼ teaspoon (1.25 g) garlic powder (optional)
- ¼ teaspoon (1.25 g) smoked paprika (optional)

Instructions

Prep Time: 10 min.   **Cooking Time:** 20 min.   **Total Time:** 30 min.   **Difficulty:** Easy

1. Preheat the oven to 300°F (150°C).
2. Wash and thoroughly dry the kale leaves. Remove the tough stems and tear the leaves into uniform-sized pieces.
3. Place the kale leaves in a large bowl. Add the olive oil and massage the leaves with your hands to ensure they are well-coated.
4. Add the sea salt, garlic powder, and smoked paprika if using. Mix well.
5. Spread the kale leaves in a single layer on a baking sheet lined with parchment paper.
6. Bake for 15-20 minutes, turning the leaves halfway through, until they are crispy and slightly golden. Be careful not to burn them.
7. Let cool and serve.

Nutritional Information per Serving (about 1 cup / 30 g)

Calories: 55; **Carbohydrates:** 7 g; **Fat:** 3 g; **Protein:** 2 g; **Saturated Fat:** 0.5 g; **Cholesterol:** 0 mg; **Sugars:** 1 g.

NOTES: You can customize the flavor of the kale chips by adding different spices, such as cayenne pepper for a spicy kick or nutritional yeast for a cheesy flavor.

Store the chips in an airtight container to keep them crispy.

6. Fresh Fruit with Almond Butter

Description

This fresh fruit with almond butter is perfect for health-conscious individuals looking for a nutritious and delicious snack. It's an excellent source of vitamins, minerals, protein, and healthy fats, perfect for an energizing break during the day.

Ingredients

- 1 medium apple, sliced
- 1 medium banana, sliced
- 1 cup (150 g) fresh strawberries, halved
- ½ cup (75 g) fresh blueberries
- ¼ cup (60 g) natural almond butter (no added sugar)
- 1 teaspoon (5 ml) honey (optional)
- A squeeze of lemon juice (to prevent apple browning)

Instructions

Prep Time: 10 min. **Cooking Time:** 0 min. **Total Time:** 10 min. **Difficulty:** Easy

1. Wash and prepare the fruit: slice the apple and banana, halve the strawberries, and leave the blueberries whole.
2. Arrange the fruit on a serving platter.
3. In a small bowl, mix the almond butter with honey (if using).
4. Drizzle the almond butter over the fruit or serve it on the side for dipping.
5. Squeeze a bit of lemon juice over the apple slices to prevent browning.
6. Serve immediately and enjoy your healthy and delicious snack.

Nutritional Information per Serving (about 1 cup / 240 ml of fruit with 2 tablespoons of almond butter)

Calories: 200; **Carbohydrates:** 35 g; **Fat:** 9 g; **Protein:** 4 g; **Saturated Fat:** 0.8 g; **Cholesterol:** 0 mg; **Sugars:** 20 g.

NOTES: You can substitute almond butter with peanut butter or another nut butter of your choice.

Add chia seeds or flaxseeds for an extra boost of fiber and omega-3.

Store prepared fruit in an airtight container in the refrigerator if not consumed immediately.

7. Steamed Edamame

Description
Steamed edamame is a perfect snack for health-conscious individuals looking for a plant-based source of protein and fiber. Easy and quick to prepare, this light dish is ideal for accompanying lunches or dinners, or as a healthy snack.

Ingredients
- 2 cups (300 g) edamame in pods
- 1 tablespoon (15 g) coarse salt
- ½ teaspoon (2.5 g) sea salt for garnish (optional)
- 1 garlic clove, minced (optional)
- 1 teaspoon (5 ml) toasted sesame oil (optional)
- 1 tablespoon (10 g) toasted sesame seeds (optional)

Instructions

Prep Time: 5 min.   **Cooking Time:** 10 min.   **Total Time:** 15 min.   **Difficulty:** Easy

1. Bring a pot of water with the coarse salt to a boil.
2. Add the edamame and cook for 5-6 minutes, until the pods are tender but still crisp.
3. Drain the edamame and rinse under cold water to stop the cooking process.
4. If desired, toss with toasted sesame oil, minced garlic, and toasted sesame seeds.
5. Sprinkle with sea salt before serving.

Nutritional Information per Serving (about 1/2 cup / 75 g)
Calories: 120; **Carbohydrates:** 10 g; **Fat:** 5 g; **Protein:** 9 g; **Saturated Fat:** 0.5 g; **Cholesterol:** 0 mg; **Sugars:** 2 g.

NOTES: Edamame can be served warm or cold, depending on preference.
Add a pinch of chili powder for a spicy kick.

8. Guacamole with Vegetable Sticks

Description
This guacamole with vegetable sticks is perfect for health-conscious individuals looking for a delicious and nutritious snack. Rich in healthy fats, vitamins, and minerals, it's ideal for a light appetizer or a fresh, crunchy snack.

Ingredients
- For the Guacamole:
- 2 ripe avocados
- 1 medium tomato, finely chopped
- ¼ red onion, finely chopped
- 1 jalapeño pepper, finely chopped (optional)
- 2 tablespoons (30 ml) fresh lime juice
- ¼ cup (10 g) fresh cilantro, chopped
- 1 garlic clove, minced
- ½ teaspoon (2.5 g) salt
- ¼ teaspoon (1.25 g) black pepper
- For the Vegetable Sticks:
- 2 carrots, cut into sticks
- 2 cucumbers, cut into sticks
- 2 bell peppers (red and yellow), cut into strips
- 1 celery stalk, cut into sticks
- 1 bunch of radishes, halved

Instructions

Prep Time: 15 min. **Cooking Time:** 0 min. **Total Time:** 15 min. **Difficulty:** Easy

1. Cut the avocados in half, remove the pit, and scoop out the flesh with a spoon. Place the flesh in a bowl.
2. Mash the avocados with a fork until creamy but still slightly chunky.
3. Add the tomato, red onion, jalapeño (if using), lime juice, cilantro, garlic, salt, and pepper. Mix well.
4. Transfer the guacamole to a serving bowl.
5. Arrange the vegetable sticks around the guacamole bowl.
6. Serve immediately to prevent the avocado from browning.

Nutritional Information per Serving (about 1/2 cup guacamole and 1 cup vegetable sticks)
Calories: 150; **Carbohydrates:** 12 g; **Fat:** 10 g; **Protein:** 2 g; **Saturated Fat:** 1.5 g; **Cholesterol:** 0 mg; **Sugars:** 4 g.

NOTES: To keep the guacamole fresh, cover it with plastic wrap in direct contact with the surface.
You can add an extra flavor touch with a pinch of cumin or cayenne pepper.

9. Parmesan Popcorn

Description

Parmesan popcorn is the perfect snack for health-conscious individuals looking for a tasty yet light option. Easy to prepare and full of flavor, it's ideal for a movie night or a crunchy break during the day.

Ingredients

- ½ cup (120 ml) popcorn kernels
- 2 tablespoons (30 ml) coconut oil or olive oil
- ¼ cup (30 g) grated Parmesan cheese
- ½ teaspoon (2.5 g) sea salt
- ¼ teaspoon (1.25 g) black pepper
- ¼ teaspoon (1.25 g) garlic powder (optional)
- ¼ teaspoon (1.25 g) sweet paprika (optional)

Instructions

Prep Time: 5 min. | **Cooking Time:** 10 min. | **Total Time:** 15 min. | **Difficulty:** Easy

1. Heat the oil in a large pot over medium-high heat. Add a couple of popcorn kernels and cover with a lid.
2. When the kernels start to pop, add the rest of the popcorn kernels in a single layer. Cover and occasionally shake the pot to ensure the kernels pop evenly.
3. Once the popping sound slows down (about 2-3 seconds between pops), remove the pot from the heat and transfer the popcorn to a large bowl.
4. Immediately sprinkle the grated Parmesan cheese, salt, black pepper, garlic powder, and sweet paprika (if using) over the hot popcorn. Toss well to ensure the seasoning is evenly distributed.
5. Serve immediately for the best flavor and crunchiness.

Nutritional Information per Serving (about 2 cups / 50 g)

Calories: 150; **Carbohydrates:** 15 g; **Fat:** 9 g; **Protein:** 4 g; **Saturated Fat:** 4 g; **Cholesterol:** 5 mg; **Sugars:** 0 g.

NOTES: You can substitute Parmesan with another low-fat grated cheese for a different flavor.
For an extra kick of flavor, add a pinch of cayenne pepper.

10. Fruit Salad

Description

This fruit salad is perfect for health-conscious individuals looking for a fresh, light, and nutritious snack. Rich in vitamins, minerals, and antioxidants, it's ideal for a healthy breakfast, a light lunch, or a dessert.

Ingredients

- 1 cup (150 g) strawberries, halved
- 1 cup (150 g) blueberries
- 1 cup (150 g) fresh pineapple, cubed
- 1 cup (150 g) mango, cubed
- 2 kiwis, peeled and sliced
- 1 orange, peeled and segmented
- 1 tablespoon (15 ml) fresh lemon juice
- 1 tablespoon (15 ml) honey or maple syrup (optional)
- Fresh mint leaves for garnish

Instructions

Prep Time: 15 min. **Cooking Time:** 0 min. **Total Time:** 15 min. **Difficulty:** Easy

1. In a large bowl, combine all the prepared fruits.
2. In a small bowl, mix the lemon juice and honey (if using).
3. Pour the lemon juice mixture over the fruit and gently toss to combine.
4. Garnish with fresh mint leaves.
5. Serve immediately or refrigerate until ready to serve.

Nutritional Information per Serving (about 1 cup / 150 g)

Calories: 90; **Carbohydrates:** 22 g; **Fat:** 0.5 g; **Protein:** 1 g; **Saturated Fat:** 0 g; **Cholesterol:** 0 mg; **Sugars:** 18 g.

NOTES: You can customize the fruit salad by adding other seasonal fruits of your choice.
For an extra flavor boost, add a pinch of cinnamon or a splash of lime juice.

Dessert Recipes

1. Avocado Chocolate Mousse

Description

This avocado chocolate mousse is perfect for health-conscious individuals looking for a rich, flavorful dessert with low saturated fat content. The avocado provides a creamy and velvety texture, while the cocoa adds an intense and delicious taste.

Ingredients

- 2 ripe avocados
- ¼ cup (60 ml) unsweetened almond milk
- ¼ cup (25 g) unsweetened cocoa powder
- ¼ cup (60 ml) maple syrup or honey
- 1 teaspoon (5 ml) vanilla extract
- A pinch of salt
- Fresh fruit and dark chocolate shavings for garnish (optional)

Instructions

Prep Time: 10 min. **Cooking Time:** 0 min. **Total Time:** 10 min. **Difficulty:** Easy

1. Cut the avocados in half, remove the pit, and scoop out the flesh with a spoon. Place the flesh in a blender or food processor.
2. Add the almond milk, cocoa powder, maple syrup, vanilla extract, and a pinch of salt.
3. Blend until smooth and creamy, scraping down the sides of the blender as needed.
4. Taste and adjust the sweetener if necessary.
5. Divide the mousse into bowls or glasses and garnish with fresh fruit and dark chocolate shavings if desired.
6. Refrigerate for at least 30 minutes before serving.

Nutritional Information per Serving (about 1/2 cup / 120 g)

Calories: 180; **Carbohydrates:** 20 g; **Fat:** 12 g; **Protein:** 2 g; **Saturated Fat:** 1.5 g; **Cholesterol:** 0 mg; **Sugars:** 12 g.

NOTES: For a vegan version, use maple syrup instead of honey.
You can add a pinch of cinnamon or chili powder for an extra flavor kick.

2. Greek Yogurt and Berries Parfait

Description
This Greek yogurt and berries parfait is perfect for health-conscious individuals looking for a high-protein, low-fat breakfast or snack. It's easy to prepare, delicious, and nutritious, making it an excellent way to start the day.

Ingredients
- 1 cup (240 ml) low-fat Greek yogurt
- ½ cup (75 g) fresh blueberries
- ½ cup (75 g) fresh raspberries
- ½ cup (75 g) strawberries, sliced
- ¼ cup (30 g) low-sugar granola
- 1 tablespoon (15 ml) honey or maple syrup (optional)
- Fresh mint leaves for garnish (optional)

Instructions

Prep Time: 10 min.   **Cooking Time:** 0 min.   **Total Time:** 10 min.   **Difficulty:** Easy

1. Start with a layer of Greek yogurt at the bottom of a glass or parfait cup.
2. Add a layer of blueberries, followed by another layer of yogurt.
3. Add a layer of raspberries, followed by another layer of yogurt.
4. Add a layer of strawberries, followed by a final layer of yogurt.
5. Sprinkle the granola on top.
6. If desired, drizzle with honey or maple syrup.
7. Garnish with fresh mint leaves.
8. Serve immediately or refrigerate until ready to serve.

Nutritional Information per Serving (about 1 cup / 240 g)
Calories: 200; **Carbohydrates:** 30 g; **Fat:** 3 g; **Protein:** 12 g; **Saturated Fat:** 1 g; **Cholesterol:** 5 mg; **Sugars:** 20 g.

NOTES: You can vary the berries depending on the season or your preferences.
For a vegan version, use soy yogurt and maple syrup.

3. Black Bean Brownies

Description

These black bean brownies are perfect for health-conscious individuals looking for a protein-rich, low-fat dessert. They are easy to make, delicious, and incredibly chocolatey, making them a guilt-free way to satisfy your sweet tooth.

Ingredients

- 1 can (15 oz / 425 g) black beans, drained and rinsed
- 3 large eggs
- ¼ cup (60 ml) melted coconut oil or olive oil
- ½ cup (50 g) unsweetened cocoa powder
- ½ cup (100 g) coconut sugar or brown sugar
- 1 teaspoon (5 ml) vanilla extract
- ½ teaspoon (2.5 g) baking powder
- A pinch of salt
- ½ cup (90 g) dark chocolate chips (optional)
- Fresh fruit or Greek yogurt for garnish (optional)

Instructions

Prep Time: 10 min. **Cooking Time:** 25 min. **Total Time:** 35 min. **Difficulty:** Easy

1. Preheat the oven to 350°F (175°C). Lightly grease an 8x8 inch (20x20 cm) square baking pan or line it with parchment paper.
2. In a blender or food processor, combine the black beans, eggs, coconut oil, cocoa powder, sugar, vanilla extract, baking powder, and salt. Blend until smooth and well combined.
3. Pour the batter into the prepared pan and spread it evenly. If desired, sprinkle the dark chocolate chips on top of the batter.
4. Bake for 20-25 minutes, or until a toothpick inserted in the center comes out clean.
5. Let the brownies cool completely in the pan before cutting into squares.
6. Serve the brownies on their own or topped with fresh fruit or Greek yogurt.

Nutritional Information per Serving (about 1 brownie)

Calories: 120; **Carbohydrates:** 18 g; **Fat:** 5 g; **Protein:** 4 g; **Saturated Fat:** 2 g; **Cholesterol:** 35 mg; **Sugars:** 10 g.

NOTES: You can substitute coconut sugar with honey or maple syrup for a natural sweetener.
For a vegan version, replace the eggs with 3 tablespoons of ground flaxseed mixed with 9 tablespoons of water.

4. Banana Ice Cream

Description

This banana ice cream is perfect for health-conscious individuals looking for a creamy, sweet dessert without added refined sugars or fats. Made with simple, natural ingredients, it's a healthy and delicious alternative to traditional ice cream.

Ingredients

- 4 ripe bananas, sliced and frozen
- ½ cup (120 ml) unsweetened almond milk (or any other plant-based milk)
- 1 teaspoon (5 ml) vanilla extract
- A pinch of salt
- Fresh fruit, dark chocolate shavings, or chopped nuts for garnish (optional)

Instructions

Prep Time: 10 min. **Cooking Time:** 0 min. **Total Time:** 10 min. **Difficulty:** Easy

1. Place the frozen banana slices in a blender or food processor.
2. Add the almond milk, vanilla extract, and a pinch of salt.
3. Blend until smooth and creamy, scraping down the sides of the blender as needed.
4. Taste and adjust the sweetness if necessary, adding a bit of honey or maple syrup if desired.
5. Serve immediately for a soft-serve consistency, or transfer to an airtight container and freeze for at least 1-2 hours for a firmer texture.
6. Garnish with fresh fruit, dark chocolate shavings, or chopped nuts before serving.

Nutritional Information per Serving (about 1/2 cup / 120 g)

Calories: 90; **Carbohydrates:** 23 g; **Fat:** 0.5 g; **Protein:** 1 g; **Saturated Fat:** 0 g; **Cholesterol:** 0 mg; **Sugars:** 14 g.

NOTES: You can add a tablespoon of peanut butter or cocoa powder for a flavor variation.
Store the ice cream in the freezer for up to one week.

5. Coconut Chia Pudding

Description
This coconut chia pudding is perfect for health-conscious individuals looking for a nutrient-rich, low-fat breakfast or snack. It's easy to make, delicious, and full of fiber, protein, and healthy fats.

Ingredients
- ¼ cup (40 g) chia seeds
- 1 cup (240 ml) unsweetened coconut milk
- 1 tablespoon (15 ml) maple syrup or honey
- ½ teaspoon (2.5 ml) vanilla extract
- A pinch of salt
- Fresh fruit, shredded coconut, and nuts for garnish (optional)

Instructions

Prep Time: 5 min. **Cooking Time:** 0 min. **Total Time:** 5 min. + 4 hours of chilling time **Difficulty:** Easy

1. In a bowl, mix together the chia seeds, coconut milk, maple syrup (or honey), vanilla extract, and a pinch of salt.
2. Stir well to ensure the chia seeds are evenly distributed and not clumping together.
3. Cover the bowl and refrigerate for at least 4 hours, or preferably overnight, until the pudding has thickened.
4. Before serving, stir the pudding well and divide into bowls or glasses.
5. Garnish with fresh fruit, shredded coconut, and nuts as desired.

Nutritional Information per Serving (about 1/2 cup / 120 g)
Calories: 180; **Carbohydrates:** 15 g; **Fat:** 10 g; **Protein:** 4 g; **Saturated Fat:** 7 g; **Cholesterol:** 0 mg; **Sugars:** 8 g.

NOTES: You can use any plant-based milk instead of coconut milk to vary the flavor and fat content.
Add a sprinkle of cocoa powder or cinnamon for an extra flavor kick.

6. Whole Wheat Apple Pie

Description
This whole wheat apple pie is perfect for health-conscious individuals who want a classic dessert made healthier. With whole wheat flour and less sugar, this pie is rich in fiber and flavor, perfect for a light dessert or snack.

Ingredients

For the Crust:
- 1½ cups (180 g) whole wheat flour
- ½ cup (120 g) cold butter, cubed
- 2-3 tablespoons (30-45 ml) ice water
- ½ teaspoon (2.5 g) salt

For the Filling:
- 6 medium apples (about 900 g), peeled, cored, and sliced
- ¼ cup (50 g) coconut sugar or brown sugar
- ¼ cup (60 ml) unsweetened apple juice
- 2 tablespoons (15 g) whole wheat flour
- 1 teaspoon (5 g) ground cinnamon
- ¼ teaspoon (1.25 g) ground nutmeg
- 1 teaspoon (5 ml) vanilla extract
- 1 tablespoon (15 ml) lemon juice

Instructions

Prep Time: 30 min. **Cooking Time:** 45 min. **Total Time:** 1 hour 15 min. **Difficulty:** Medium

For the Crust:
1. In a large bowl, mix the whole wheat flour and salt.
2. Add the cold butter and use a pastry cutter or two knives to work the butter into the flour until the mixture resembles coarse crumbs with pea-sized pieces of butter.
3. Add the ice water one tablespoon at a time, mixing until the dough comes together.
4. Form the dough into a disk, wrap in plastic wrap, and refrigerate for at least 30 minutes.

For the Filling:
1. In a large bowl, mix the sliced apples with the coconut sugar, apple juice, whole wheat flour, cinnamon, nutmeg, vanilla extract, and lemon juice.
2. Let sit for about 15 min. to allow the flavors to meld.

Assembly:
1. Preheat the oven to 375°F (190°C).
2. On a lightly floured surface, roll out half of the dough into a 12-inch (30 cm) circle. Transfer the dough to a 9-inch (23 cm) pie dish.
3. Pour the apple filling into the crust, spreading it evenly.
4. Roll out the other half of the dough and cover the filling. Seal the edges and cut slits in the top to allow steam to escape.
5. Bake for 45 min., or until the crust is golden and the filling is bubbling.
6. Let the pie cool completely before serving.

Nutritional Information per Serving (about 1 slice)
Calories: 250; **Carbohydrates:** 38 g; **Fat:** 10 g; **Protein:** 3 g; **Saturated Fat:** 6 g; **Cholesterol:** 25 mg; **Sugars:** 15 g.

NOTES: You can add a handful of chopped nuts or raisins to the filling for extra texture.
For a vegan version, replace the butter with solid coconut oil.

7. Blueberry Muffins

Description
These blueberry muffins are perfect for health-conscious individuals looking for a light and nutritious treat. Made with whole wheat flour and less sugar, these muffins are rich in fiber and flavor, ideal for a healthy breakfast or snack.

Ingredients
- 1½ cups (180 g) whole wheat flour
- ½ cup (100 g) brown sugar
- ½ teaspoon (2.5 g) baking soda
- ½ teaspoon (2.5 g) baking powder
- ¼ teaspoon (1.25 g) salt
- ½ cup (120 ml) unsweetened almond milk
- ¼ cup (60 ml) melted coconut oil or olive oil
- 2 large eggs
- 1 teaspoon (5 ml) vanilla extract
- 1 cup (150 g) fresh or frozen blueberries
- 1 tablespoon (10 g) whole wheat flour (for coating the blueberries)

Instructions

Prep Time: 15 min.   **Cooking Time:** 20-25 min.   **Total Time:** 40 min.   **Difficulty:** Easy

1. Preheat the oven to 375°F (190°C). Line a muffin tin with paper liners or lightly grease it.
2. In a large bowl, whisk together the whole wheat flour, brown sugar, baking soda, baking powder, and salt.
3. In another bowl, beat together the almond milk, coconut oil, eggs, and vanilla extract until smooth.
4. Pour the wet ingredients into the dry ingredients and mix gently until just combined. Do not overmix.
5. In a small bowl, toss the blueberries with 1 tablespoon of whole wheat flour to prevent them from sinking in the batter.
6. Gently fold the blueberries into the batter.
7. Divide the batter evenly among the muffin cups, filling them about 2/3 full.
8. Bake for 20-25 minutes, or until a toothpick inserted into the center comes out clean.
9. Let the muffins cool in the tin for 5 minutes, then transfer them to a wire rack to cool completely.

Nutritional Information per Muffin
Calories: 160; **Carbohydrates:** 25 g; **Fat:** 6 g; **Protein:** 3 g; **Saturated Fat:** 3 g; **Cholesterol:** 35 mg; **Sugars:** 10 g.

NOTES: You can substitute coconut oil with sunflower oil for a lighter version.
Add a handful of chopped nuts for extra crunch and flavor.

8. Fruit Crumble

Description

This fruit crumble is perfect for health-conscious individuals looking for a delicious and nutritious dessert. Made with whole wheat flour and less sugar, this crumble is rich in fiber and flavor, ideal for a healthy breakfast or light dessert.

Ingredients

- For the Filling:
- 4 cups (600 g) mixed fruit (apples, pears, berries)
- 2 tablespoons (30 ml) lemon juice
- ¼ cup (50 g) coconut sugar or brown sugar
- 1 teaspoon (5 g) ground cinnamon
- 1 tablespoon (10 g) whole wheat flour
- For the Crumble:
- 1 cup (120 g) whole wheat flour
- ½ cup (45 g) rolled oats
- ¼ cup (50 g) coconut sugar or brown sugar
- ¼ cup (60 ml) melted coconut oil or cold butter, cubed
- ½ teaspoon (2.5 g) ground cinnamon
- A pinch of salt

Instructions

Prep Time: 15 min. **Cooking Time:** 30-35 min. **Total Time:** 50 min. **Difficulty:** Easy

1. Preheat the oven to 350°F (175°C). Lightly grease a 9x9 inch (23x23 cm) baking dish or similar.
2. In a large bowl, mix the mixed fruit with the lemon juice, coconut sugar, cinnamon, and whole wheat flour. Transfer the fruit mixture to the prepared baking dish.
3. In another bowl, mix together the whole wheat flour, rolled oats, coconut sugar, cinnamon, and salt. Add the melted coconut oil (or butter) and mix until the mixture is crumbly.
4. Evenly distribute the crumble mixture over the fruit.
5. Bake for 30-35 minutes, or until the fruit filling is bubbly and the crumble is golden brown.
6. Let cool slightly before serving.

Nutritional Information per Serving (about 1/8 of the crumble)

Calories: 180; **Carbohydrates:** 30 g; **Fat:** 7 g; **Protein:** 3 g; **Saturated Fat:** 4 g; **Cholesterol:** 0 mg; **Sugars:** 15 g.

NOTES: You can use any combination of seasonal fruits for this crumble.
Add a handful of chopped nuts to the crumble for extra crunch and flavor.

9. Coconut Panna Cotta

Description

This coconut panna cotta is perfect for health-conscious individuals looking for a creamy and light dessert. Made with coconut milk and natural sweeteners, it's a delicious and easy-to-make treat, ideal for ending a meal on a healthy note.

Ingredients

- 1 can (13.5 oz / 400 ml) unsweetened coconut milk
- ¼ cup (60 ml) unsweetened almond milk
- 2 tablespoons (30 ml) maple syrup or honey
- 1 teaspoon (5 ml) vanilla extract
- 1 packet (2¼ tsp / 7 g) unflavored gelatin powder
- 3 tablespoons (45 ml) cold water
- Fresh fruit and coconut flakes for garnish (optional)

Instructions

Prep Time: 10 min.	Cooking Time: 5 min.	Chilling Time: 4 h	Total Time: 4 h 15 min.	Difficulty: Easy

1. In a small bowl, sprinkle the gelatin over the cold water and let it soften for about 5 minutes.
2. In a medium saucepan, heat the coconut milk and almond milk over medium heat until it starts to simmer. Do not boil.
3. Add the maple syrup (or honey) and vanilla extract to the milk mixture and stir well.
4. Remove the saucepan from the heat and add the softened gelatin. Stir until the gelatin is completely dissolved.
5. Pour the mixture into individual molds or glasses. Let cool to room temperature, then cover and refrigerate for at least 4 hours, or until set.
6. Before serving, garnish with fresh fruit and coconut flakes, if desired.

Nutritional Information per Serving (about 1/2 cup / 120 g)

Calories: 150; **Carbohydrates:** 10 g; **Fat:** 12 g; **Protein:** 2 g; **Saturated Fat:** 10 g; **Cholesterol:** 0 mg; **Sugars:** 8 g.

NOTES: You can substitute almond milk with any other plant-based milk of your choice.
For a vegan version, use agar-agar instead of gelatin.

10. Oat and Banana Cookies

Description
These oat and banana cookies are perfect for health-conscious individuals looking for a nutritious and delicious snack. Made without added sugars and with simple ingredients, they are ideal for a quick breakfast or a healthy snack.

Ingredients
- 2 ripe bananas, mashed
- 1½ cups (150 g) rolled oats
- ¼ cup (60 ml) unsweetened almond milk
- ¼ cup (60 g) natural peanut butter
- 1 teaspoon (5 ml) vanilla extract
- ½ teaspoon (2.5 g) ground cinnamon
- ¼ cup (30 g) chopped nuts (optional)
- ¼ cup (40 g) dark chocolate chips (optional)

Instructions

Prep Time: 10 min.   **Cooking Time:** 15 min.   **Total Time:** 25 min.   **Difficulty:** Easy

1. Preheat the oven to 350°F (175°C) and line a baking sheet with parchment paper.
2. In a large bowl, mix the mashed bananas, almond milk, peanut butter, and vanilla extract until smooth.
3. Add the rolled oats and ground cinnamon, mixing until well combined.
4. Stir in the chopped nuts and dark chocolate chips, if using.
5. Using a spoon, drop the batter onto the prepared baking sheet, forming cookies about 2 inches (5 cm) in diameter.
6. Bake for 15 minutes, or until the edges are lightly golden.
7. Allow the cookies to cool on the baking sheet for 5 minutes, then transfer them to a wire rack to cool completely.

Nutritional Information per Cookie (about 1 cookie)
Calories: 90; **Carbohydrates:** 15 g; **Fat:** 3 g; **Protein:** 2 g; **Saturated Fat:** 1 g; **Cholesterol:** 0 mg; **Sugars:** 5 g.

NOTES: You can add dried fruit or seeds to boost the nutritional value.
Store the cookies in an airtight container for up to a week.

Conclusion

Dear Readers,

Congratulations! You have reached the end of this culinary journey through "The Low Cholesterol Cookbook." I hope you have found inspiration, delight, and perhaps some new culinary wisdom. You have explored a world of exquisite and healthy dishes, from fresh and crunchy salads to comforting soups, all the way to desserts that make your heart smile without weighing on your conscience.

In these pages, you have learned to cook with love and care, to choose ingredients that nourish not just the body but also the soul. You have discovered that eating healthy does not mean sacrificing taste; indeed, it can be a refined art, a dance of flavors that makes you feel alive and vibrant.

And now, the serious part: reviews. Yes, indeed! If there's one thing Oscar Wilde taught us, it's that others' opinions can be both a blessing and a curse. But in this case, we sincerely hope it's the former. Your reviews not only make us blush with joy or cry with emotion but also help us grow, improve, and most importantly, continue to bring you content you love.

So, don't be shy! Take a moment to share your thoughts, your impressions, and yes, even your constructive criticisms. We are here to listen and learn from you. Your feedback is our yeast, our secret spice, our magic ingredient.

Thank you from the bottom of our hearts for reading this book, for trying our recipes, and for being part of our culinary community. Always remember: life is too short to eat badly, and too precious not to take care of yourself.

With affection and a pinch of irony,

Index

A
- almond butter — 65
- Almond butter — 83
- Almond flour — 83
- almond milk — 61, 70, 73, 76, 78, 79
- Almond milk — 83
- almonds — 58, 63
- Almonds — 83
- apple cider vinegar — 56, 58
- Apple cider vinegar — 83
- apples — 75, 77
- Apples — 83
- asparagus — 57, 59
- Asparagus — 5, 6, 83
- avocado — 56, 58, 67, 70
- Avocado — 5, 6, 56, 70, 83

B
- banana — 61, 65, 73, 79
- Banana — 5, 6, 73, 79, 83
- bananas — 63, 73, 79
- Bananas — 83
- Barley — 5, 83
- basil — 55
- Basil — 83
- bell pepper — 53, 57, 59
- Bell pepper — 83
- bell peppers — 56, 58, 67
- Bell peppers — 83
- black beans — 53, 72
- Black beans — 83
- blueberries — 63, 65, 69, 71, 76
- Blueberries — 83
- breadcrumbs — 55
- Breadcrumbs — 83
- broccoli — 59
- Broccoli — 83
- brown sugar — 72, 75, 76, 77
- Brown sugar — 83

C
- Cannellini beans — 83
- carrot — 55, 59
- Carrot — 5, 83
- carrots — 53, 56, 57, 58, 67
- Carrots — 83
- celery — 67
- Celery — 83
- cherry — 56, 57, 58
- Cherry — 83
- chia seeds — 61, 63, 65, 74
- Chia seeds — 83
- Chicken breast — 83
- chickpeas — 60
- Chickpeas — 83
- cinnamon — 69, 70, 74, 75, 77, 79
- Cinnamon — 83
- cocoa powder — 70, 72, 73, 74
- Cocoa powder — 83
- coconut milk — 74, 78
- Coconut milk — 83
- coconut oil — 68, 72, 75, 76, 77
- Coconut oil — 83
- Cod fillet — 83
- Coriander — 83
- Corn tortilla — 83
- Couscous — 5, 83
- cucumber — 56, 58
- Cucumber — 83

D
- dark chocolate chips — 72, 79
- Dark chocolate chips — 83
- dates — 62
- Dates — 83
- Dill — 83

E
- edamame — 66
- Edamame — 6, 66, 83

- egg 55
- Egg 5, 83
- Eggplant 83
- eggs 72, 76
- Eggs 83

F
- Fajitas spice mix 83
- Feta cheese 83
- flaxseed 72
- Flaxseed 83
- fresh 56, 61
- Fresh 83

G
- garlic 53, 54, 55, 56, 57, 58, 59, 60, 64, 66, 67, 68
- Garlic 83
- gelatin 78
- Gelatin 83
- ginger 59
- Ginger 83
- Grated 83
- Greek yogurt 61, 63, 71, 72, 83
- Green apple 83
- Ground 83

H
- honey 61, 62, 63, 65, 69, 70, 71, 72, 73, 74, 78
- Honey 5, 6, 63, 83

K
- kale 58, 64
- Kale 6, 58, 64, 83
- Kiwi 83

L
- lemon juice 57, 58, 60, 65, 69, 75, 77
- Lemon juice 83
- lemon zest 54
- Lemon zest 83
- lentils 55
- Lentils 83
- Lettuce 83
- lime 53, 56, 67, 69
- Lime 83

M
- maple syrup 59, 61, 62, 69, 70, 71, 72, 73, 74, 78
- Maple syrup 83
- Minced turkey 83
- mint leaves 69, 71
- Mint leaves 83
- Mixed berries 83
- mixed mushrooms 54
- Mixed mushrooms 83

O
- oats 77, 79
- Oats 5, 83
- olive oil 53, 54, 55, 56, 57, 58, 59, 60, 64, 68, 72, 76
- Olive oil 83
- onion 53, 54, 55, 56, 57, 59, 67
- Onion 83
- orange 69
- Orange 83
- oregano 53, 55, 57
- Oregano 83

P
- Parmesan cheese 54, 55, 68, 83
- parsley 54, 57, 60
- Parsley 83
- pears 77
- Pears 83
- peeled 55
- Peeled 83
- Pine nuts 83
- popcorn kernels 68
- Popcorn kernels 83
- Pumpkin seeds 83

Q
- quinoa 58
- Quinoa 5, 6, 58, 83

R
- raisins 22, 24, 58, 75, 81
- Red 83
- Red cabbage 83
- Ripe 83
- Rolled 83
- Rosemary 83

S
- Salmon fillet 83
- salt 53, 54, 55, 56, 57, 58, 59, 60, 64, 66, 67, 68, 70, 72, 73, 74, 75, 76, 77
- Salt 53, 54, 55, 56, 57, 58, 83
- Sea 83
- sesame oil 66

- Sesame oil — 83
- sesame seeds — 59, 66
- Sesame seeds — 59, 83
- Smoked salmon — 83
- Soy sauce (low-sodium) — 83
- Spelt — 5, 83
- spinach — 54, 59
- Spinach — 5, 6, 83
- strawberries — 63, 65, 69, 71
- Strawberries — 83
- sugar — 55
- sunflower seeds — 62
- Sunflower seeds — 83

T
- tahini — 60
- Tahini — 83
- Thyme — 83
- tofu — 59
- Tofu — 5, 6, 59, 83
- tomato — 53, 55, 67
- Tomato — 5, 55, 83
- tomatoes — 53
- Tomatoes — 83
- Turkey (minced) — 83
- Turmeric — 83

V
- vanilla extract — 62, 63, 70, 72, 73, 74, 75, 76, 78, 79
- Vanilla extract — 83
- vegetable broth — 54
- Vegetable broth — 83

W
- walnuts — 63
- Walnuts — 83
- water — 55, 58, 60, 62, 66, 72, 75, 78
- Water — 83
- Whole granola — 83
- Whole wheat bagel — 83
- Whole wheat bread — 83
- whole wheat flour — 75, 76, 77
- Whole wheat flour — 83
- Whole wheat tortilla — 83

Z
- zucchini — 53, 57, 59
- Zucchini — 6, 83

1° BONUS

Weekly food diary

2° BONUS

Printable Shopping List

Made in the USA
Las Vegas, NV
06 February 2025